P9-BYM-327

To
Spafford Ackerly, M.D.

BX
1475.9
.02

ON BECOMING CHILDREN OF GOD

On Becoming
Children of God

by Wayne E. Oates

Published for
The Cooperative Publication Association
by
The Westminster Press
Philadelphia

COPYRIGHT © MCMLXIX THE WESTMINSTER PRESS

All rights reserved—no part of this book may be reproduced in any form without permission in writing from the publisher, except by a reviewer who wishes to quote brief passages in connection with a review in magazine or newspaper.

Scripture quotations from the Revised Standard Version of the Bible are copyright, 1946 and 1952 by the Division of Christian Education of the National Council of Churches, and are used by permission.

STANDARD BOOK NO. 664–21281–6
LIBRARY OF CONGRESS CATALOG CARD NO. 68–20149

Acknowledgment for permission to reprint quotations is made to the following publishers:

Doubleday & Company, Inc., for *The Diary of a Young Girl,* by Anne Frank. 1952.

Harcourt, Brace & World, Inc., for *The Little Prince,* by Antoine de Saint-Exupéry, copyright, 1943, by Harcourt, Brace & World, Inc.

Published by The Westminster Press ®
Philadelphia, Pennsylvania
PRINTED IN THE UNITED STATES OF AMERICA

PREFACE

THIS BOOK is written for adult teachers of children and youth. Yet I have written it hopeful that the young person who reads it might get much self-understanding. We have too many "trade secrets" as adults. We should share them with youths who are willing to take the time to hear us. I have not put anything in these pages that I would not also be willing for my own sons (ages fifteen and twenty) to read and "quiz" me on.

I am indebted to my sons and their mother for having taught me much of what is in these pages. The experienced psychologist of personality will immediately recognize my debt to Spafford Ackerly, Gordon Allport, András Angyal, Erik Erikson, Jean Piaget, Lewis J. Sherrill, and Harry Stack Sullivan for my conceptual hypotheses. The end result, however, is my own making. For better or for worse, it is my responsibility.

W. E. O.

Louisville, Kentucky

CONTENTS

Chapter I

BECOMING CHILDREN OF GOD

THE VERY TITLE of this book can be challenged. The challenger will ask: Do we *become* children of God? Shouldn't one say that we *are* children of God? Is not Christ the light that lights every man that comes into the world? If so, how then can we *become* children of God?

If I am honest with such a challenger, I would have to say: Yes. We *are* children of God. We are created in his image. We are made in his likeness. He has made us for himself. We are called the children of God. So we are. By creation we are planned to be children of God.

When I have answered my challenger this way, however, something yet needs to be said. These truths which he holds to be self-evident must themselves be placed under the microscope. They must be examined in detail. That is the purpose of this book. When we do this, in fact, a whole new world of perception appears.

Other more serious questions are prompted by my challenger's affirmation. For example, we know that we are created in God's image. But *when* is that creation an accomplished fact? At conception? At birth? At "the age of accountability"? Or is that creation ever finished short of the resurrection? We know that Christ is the light that lights every man who comes into the world. But, is that light not incarnated first in parents? Then does it not gradually dawn in the direct awareness of the individual himself as a self before God? Does it not more fully appear in the community of the larger family of mankind known as the church, the body of Christ? God has made us for himself, but our hearts are restless until they rest in him. Whence comes this anxiety and restlessness? Such questions as these are the finer detail with which this book is concerned.

Both sets of questions are valid. They stand as paradoxes in relation to each other. On close examination mankind is a bundle of contradictions. On closer examination man is a variegated spectrum of color. Man is not a cleft set of either/or, black or white, easy distinctions. He is a complex, not a simple, creature. Any accurate account of our nature must take into consideration both the completeness and the incompleteness of our being and our becoming. We *are* the children of God. Yet we are in the process of becoming the children of God too. Creation continues in the course and process of human life. One of the purposes of this book is to trace in detail that process of becoming, to appreciate the nuances and shades of the marvelous spectrum of our nature.

The family and the church are the mothering-fathering relationships into which God sends an infant. God sets him on the pilgrimage of being and becoming a child of God. The pattern and design of this book is to bring the reader to grips with the human events in that process whereby we indeed and in fact become that which in possibility we are as children of God. This tension between potentiality in relation to God and actuality in relation to God is held taut by the writer of The First Letter of John when he says:

> See what love the Father has given us, that we should be called children of God; and so we are. The reason why the world does not know us is that it did not know him. Beloved, we are God's children now; it does not yet appear what we shall be, but we know that when he appears we shall be like him, for we shall see him as he is. And every one who thus hopes in him purifies himself as he is pure. (I John 3:1–3.)

Any person who is a parent has at hand in his own relationship to his children a very human illustration of the tension and the hope described by the writer of I John. He knows that his child is a child of God. Yet he does not know how that child will "turn out," what that child will "become."

The very word "become" is derived from an Anglo-Saxon word meaning "to come to" or "to happen." Another meaning is "to come to be," as a caterpillar becomes a butterfly. Philosophically it means to change or develop. If we add the preposition "of" to mean "become of," we introduce the element of destiny, of fate, of ultimate outcome. If we use the word "becoming," we refer to that which is appropriate, suitable, befitting, such as "becoming" and "unbecoming" behavior.

Therefore, wrapped up in the homely illustration of the relationship of a parent to a child and in the varieties of meaning in the word "become" and "becoming" are all three tenses of time: (1) the established fact of our having come into being as an accomplished event from the past; (2) the present process of change that is taking place now; and (3) the ultimate fate of that which we are yet "to become."

This book is addressed to teachers who work at relating the gospel to the contemporary experience of young people in their weekday lives. They work at enabling young people both to appreciate and to evaluate their heritage from their home and church. They labor to set the brilliant diamond of the young person's high school and elementary education in the setting of their loyalty to God and their church.

Furthermore, this book is written to parents who seek to understand themselves as parents. Self-knowledge enables parents to appreciate their relationship to their children as it is rooted and grounded in their relationship to God.

Hopefully, this book will become a guide, also, for young people. They think about themselves as selves. They are seeking to put away childish things. How can they do this without losing their spontaneity and their childlike quality? How can they enter adulthood without it becoming a "shade of the prison-house" to shut out the heaven that lies about us in our infancy? How can the work of adulthood become as the play of childhood? The young person is an emerging young adult called to the dialogues of business, love, and strife. How can he bring to this the heaven-born freedom of a little child and yet maintain the serious intention of mature adulthood? This is his conflict. My hope is that these pages may be an inspiration to young persons, teachers, and parents, providing a basis of common understanding between them to the end that they all together may "glorify God and enjoy him forever."

Chapter II

THE SOURCE
OF HUMAN PERSONALITY: FAITH

THE HUMAN BEING is the most unfinished of creatures at the time of his birth. Just before I started this paragraph I visited the Children's Hospital in my city. I went with a close friend to visit his newly born granddaughter. She was born six weeks prematurely. She is now in an incubator, being brought to that level of completion she would have been at if she had not been born prematurely. Even then she and the other babies in the nursery will be far more incomplete than any other of the creatures of earth. A baby at birth cannot lift its head, turn over, find food for itself, or walk. A human infant takes longer to develop these capacities than lower animals. During this lengthened period of infancy, a greatly unfinished creation is given to parents by God. They are invited, urged, and required as colaborers with God to join in the "finishing of his new creation" of a human person. As Walt Whitman says of the child:

> His own parents, he that father'd him and she that
>   conceived him in her womb and birthed,
> They gave this child more of themselves than that,
> They gave him afterward every day—they and of them
>   became part of him.[1]

FAITH: THE SOURCE OF PERSONALITY

The source of human personality is both obscure and plainly evident. The plainest source is faith. This is true in each of the many dimensions of human personality. An infant learns to do things for himself when the parent believes in him enough to let him try and enables the child to believe that he can do so too. When a person becomes a Christian, he lays hold of new sources of confidence both in himself and in God. That person in turn believes that through Christ he can become one of the children of God. As the Fourth Gospel puts it: "But to all who received him, who believed in his name, he gave power to become children of God" (John 1:12). Faith as the source of personality is more than a set of abstract propositions that can be written down on paper. Faith is confidence— in others, oneself, and God. Faith is trust—in others, oneself, and God. Faith is the stuff of which the hopes by which we live are made. As such, faith is the beginning of being a person.

Making such a statement is easy. Making it clear and evident is not. Personality begins in faith in at least three ways. First, parents launch into the unknown when they conceive a child. The more responsible they are, the more faith is required to begin a human life at the time of conception. Parents cannot do this alone. As a biological event in human life, it cannot take place without communion of some sort between a man and woman. The whole of society, along with a man and a woman, takes responsibility for a child. Therefore, legal and social requirements surround the event of birth. As an experience blessed by God, the birth of a child takes place in the household covenant of faith in God.

Second, personality begins in the faith that mother and father have in each other. They *entrust* themselves to each other in parenthood. The woman and mother, particularly, is the "vessel" of childbearing. She is placed in a vulnerable situation of helplessness during the time of pregnancy. She is called upon to trust her husband in a way that requires him to create a considerate atmosphere of trust. Together they are joint heirs in the grace of life. Suspicion and distrust are the rust and moth that destroy the life of faith. Nowhere do these deterrents to the life of faith appear more subtly or more obviously than in the conception of a child. Nowhere are openness and trust, confidence and faith, more required.

Third, the child himself is born into this atmosphere of

either faith or fear, trust or mistrust. "Most young animals," says Margaret Ribble, "can satisfy their primal hungers at birth or soon after without much assistance." The rhesus monkey even assists with his own birth and "climbs to the breast and clings with arms around . . . [his mother's] body or neck. Yet our human babies are not able to reach for mother until they are four or five months old." On the basis of this, Dr. Ribble says that "the baby is a potential person, but in the beginning is quite helpless, and his mother must actually function for him for many weeks."[2] Therefore, says Dr. Ribble, the first *right* of an infant is to a trustworthy mother. Neglect of the human element of mothering lays the foundations of insecurity, distrust, and deprivation. Faith, at the very organic level, is the assurance that the mother is *there*.

Faith and the Communication of Trust

It seems strange to use the word "faith" with reference to a little baby. One could use the word "confidence." The best word is "trust." An infant can be said to be trusting. We assume a lot when we say that he has faith. Yet there is a direct line of communication between parent and child, the parent with faith and the child in need of trust. One of the wisest psychologists of our day, Erik Erikson, sees basic trust as "an attitude toward oneself derived from the experiences of the first year of life." By basic trust he means a simple sense of trustworthiness as far as oneself is concerned. He does not necessarily mean a conscious experience, and, therefore, he uses the word "basic." We could use the term "a sense of trust." This is almost a neurological if not a completely bodily experience. In plain Anglo-Saxon it means that the child is either "at ease" or "uneasy." Every untutored mother and grandmother knows what this is. They respond to it with reassurance, comfort, warmth, and mutuality. Yet they do not sit down and think this out before they do so. They just do.

Even as the mother and grandmother can sense a child's need for reassurance and relief of his insecurity, the child can, without the necessity of words, sense who it is that understands, appreciates, and accepts him as a person with feelings and a need for trustworthy adults around him. Such people stimulate trust in him that is far deeper than verbal formulations of creeds about God. Even into adulthood, this silent level of trust in God somehow must be conveyed in religious instruction. Without it, such instruction, however sophisticated, may be like sounding brass and a tinkling cymbal.

Erikson wisely relates this need of a child for basic trust to religious faith. He asks whether the personal religion of a given family "creates the kind of faith and conviction which permeates a parent's personality and thus reenforces the child's basic trust and the world's trustworthiness."[3] He challenges all those who are religious by saying: "Whoever says he has religion must derive a faith from it which is transmitted to infants in the form of basic trust; whosoever claims that he does not need religion must derive such basic faith from elsewhere."[4]

Thus faith, abiding in the parent, is transmitted to the child in the form of basic trust. Individual mistrust is the opposite of this and it is evil. Lack of confidence of parents, the pointlessness and the faithlessness they experience—these are the sources of the denial and destruction of personality.

FAITH AND THE STRUGGLE OF THE SOUL

The fledgling personality, as well as all those who are older, experiences a struggle of the soul, and personality is created through the courageous overcoming of the fear of the unknown, the fear of growth, and the risks of suffering. All of these are involved at each stage of growth. As Lewis Sherrill says, "The infant emerges from the physical womb, but the psyche can decide only after prolonged struggle whether to emerge from the womb of safety or to stay enmeshed within it." The birth experience becomes a symbol for all life's later crises of growth. A baby is thrust out of the security, warmth, and dependence of a womb of safety. He is thrust into the insecurity of times of testing, decision, and challenge. As he accepts this challenge, he expresses faith in himself, in others, and in God. If he shrinks back, the very faith that calls for him to move ahead into the face of life is nullified. The Letter to the Hebrews puts it this way:

Therefore do not throw away your confidence, which has a great reward. For you have need of endurance, so that you may do the will of God and receive what is promised.

> For yet a little while,
> and the coming one shall come and shall not tarry;
> but my righteous one shall live by faith,
> and if he shrinks back,
> my soul has no pleasure in him.
> (Heb. 10:35–38.)

Sherrill wisely says that these challenges come again and again in life. The initial challenge to the infant is to become an individual in his own right. His parents, by their faith, enable him to do this through the trust they engender. If they as parents shrink back, they open the way to rebellion against God as some modern theologians say.[5]

FAITH: FINDING A PLACE AND QUITTING A PLACE

When you watch a little child breathe, you see him breathe out and breathe in, just like you do. When you watch a teenager coming out of the football game and sitting down on the bench, he breathes out and he breathes in, just like you do. When you watch an old person sitting on the park bench in a large city, he breathes out and he breathes in, just like you do. There is a rhythm to breathing. Faith is pictured in this rhythm. If you were to watch a child being born, you would see him moving out of the safety of the mother's womb. You would see doctors and nurses helping him by moving him into a place where he can be still. This is a symbol of the life of faith. We are always quitting a place and at the same time we are always looking for a new place. This restlessness is the nature of life itself. However, leaving a place of security calls for faith, and finding a place that is new calls for a faith that is the substance for the hopes that one has for a new place. The air one breathes, "breathing room," symbolizes this "sigh of relief" at having found oneself at home where one is.

Paul Tournier subtitles a recent volume of his called *Man and His Place* (yet unpublished in English) *Psychology and Faith*. This Swiss psychotherapist describes life in terms of faith and personality as springing from faith. When one plunges into the depths of anxiety of child, man, or woman, one finds that it is hard to question: "Can I find my place in the world? Can I know my place in the world? Is there a place in the world for me that is uniquely mine and into which no one can intrude?" These questions involve the whole person. They put into flesh all the events of one's existence. But, on the other hand, a person does not only ask these questions. He asks also: "Where am I going from here? What are we going to do now?" The purpose of the teacher of young people in the search for a place and the need to be "clued in on the move" is, therefore, twofold: First, to help them find their "place" in life and, second, to enable them to find their directions in going out on an adventure for another place in life. Likewise, the teacher is a "bridge" for persons. He or she supports and sustains growing persons as they leap from one situation and take hold of another situation in life. Tournier describes this with a different metaphor: the parable of the trapeze artist. The trapeze bar is held tightly. Another swinging bar is timed with it. The trapeze artist lets go of one bar at just the right time and takes hold of the other. To do this takes faith in life, courage to leap, and the capacity to bear the anxiety in between. Personality grows just like this. As one lets go of one "place" or "secure dwelling place" and moves to another, faith inspires courage to act. In this sense, faith is the source of personality. Life itself is maintained this way.

FAITH AND THE TEACHABLE MOMENTS OF LIFE

The breathtaking moment of the trapeze artist is a "mid-situation" that cannot be undertaken alone. It calls for a "faith community" of support and supply, preparation and nurture, commitment and consideration. Personality likewise does not form in a vacuum. It comes to be in the context of a faith community. These moments of breathtaking "in between-ness" call for courage and initiative on the part of the individual. They are teachable moments for the faith community of the family, school, and church around the individual.

For example, there is a time for a little baby to be cuddled and held in his mother's and father's arms. Yet there is a time also for him to begin to walk. As he does this he exercises courage, confidence in himself, and initiative. However, around him must be the encouragement, support, and strengthening belief of his parents. They too must believe that he can do it. As he learns to walk, therefore, his newfound skill blends his own confidence in himself with their faith in him. Such is true of all the great teachable moments of life.

The psychologist who has taught us most about this is Robert Havighurst. He says that "teachable moment" is the concept of "timing" of educational efforts. A poorly timed educational effort is wasted. He says:

> When the body is ripe, and society requires, and the self is ready to achieve a certain task, the teachable moment has come. Efforts at teaching which would have been largely wasted if they had come earlier give gratifying results when they come at the *teachable moment*, when the task should be learned.[6]

Of course the writer of the wise sayings of Ecclesiastes had a keen sense of the timing of things when he said:

> For everything there is a season, and a time for every matter under heaven:
>
> a time to be born, and a time to die;
> a time to plant, and a time to pluck up what is planted;
> a time to kill, and a time to heal;
> a time to break down, and a time to build up;
> a time to weep, and a time to laugh;
> a time to mourn, and a time to dance;
> a time to cast away stones, and a time to gather stones
>   together;
> a time to embrace, and a time to refrain from embracing;
> a time to seek, and a time to lose;
> a time to keep, and a time to cast away;
> a time to rend, and a time to sew;
> a time to keep silence, and a time to speak;
> a time to love, and a time to hate;
> a time for war, and a time for peace.
>
> (Eccl. 3:1–8.)

Therefore, the teacher who would be wise as well as informed is the one who is disciplined to "time" what is being taught with the particular events that the persons in his class are "up against" at a given time in their lives. We too often see the pupil before us as an empty cup, sitting without motion while we fill it up. Or, we see younger persons as lumps of damp but quickly drying clay that must be molded to fit our desire before it is too late. Or, to use a third figure of speech, we parents and teachers tend to see young people as a mirror in which is to be reflected our own image to the end that they will become what we would like to think we are. God never intended that these things be so. Rather, we should see those whom we teach as personalities in the making through faith. They are volatile, alive, and capable of decision. They respond to life's challenges with faith and become what their faith decisions make them. They are not cups to be filled, clay to be molded, or mirrors for our vanity. They are persons in their own right. They are emerging selves in the making through the power of faith. They come to moments of decision. They are challenged to leave earlier securities and to "go out by faith," not knowing where they go. They may "shrink back" into a false security, fail to grow, and lose integrity in the process. Teaching is the "timely" and faithful participation in these moments.

In this respect, young persons are no different from persons of any other age. The "developmental tasks" and teachable moments themselves are different, but the claims of faith are the same. Together we can pray the prayer of the psalmist: "Teach us to number our days that we may get a heart of wisdom" (Ps. 90:12).

The remainder of this volume will be devoted to a careful inspection of the nature of the most typical teachable moments that occur in the lives of young persons from birth through their senior year in high school. Similar studies could be made of the life of the teacher himself or herself. A companion volume about the "developmental tasks" of the teacher's life would be helpful. The purpose of this volume, however, is to explore in detail the process of "becoming children of God." Both a psychological and a theological perspective are necessary. If we can together get a heart of wisdom, then the particular techniques and procedures for implementing that wisdom will tend to be born out of the wisdom itself. This book aims to develop in the teacher an appreciation of the things young persons are "up against," the kinds of decisions they necessarily must make. Thus, the ways can appear in which a teacher can participate with them as an understanding adult through the processes of teaching and fellowship.

"Teach Us What We Are to Do"

The Christian teacher seeks that all persons—himself, his pupil, parents of his pupil—be aware of God. God discloses himself to us. He reveals himself to us in his redeeming love in Jesus Christ. We respond to him in faith and love, hopefully. This is a response of faith. The response of faith enables us all —teachers, pupils, and parents—to know who we are as sons of God. This faith roots us in the Christian community. This faith enlivens us in the Spirit of God and every relationship. This faith enables us to fulfill our common discipleship in the world. This faith secures us as we abide in the Christian hope.

The experience recorded in Judg., ch. 13, about Manoah and his wife, occurred before the revelation of God in Jesus Christ. Nevertheless, this man and woman were aware of God as he appeared to them in his messengers. They responded to him in communion with his messengers. They saw in "the man of God who came to them" the very countenance of God. They were filled with awe and wonder.

Manoah, the father of the child to be born, namely Samson, entreated the Lord and said: "O, Lord, I pray thee, let the man of God whom thou didst send come again to us, and teach us what we are to do with the boy that will be born."

The Scripture tells us that "God listened to the voice of Manoah." The teacher today is one who guides the young in the process of becoming a person in his own right before God. The shape of what a young person is in fact to become is not known. That shape is built on faith. Yet that faith, of teacher, pupil, and parent, itself has much to do with determining "what we are to do with the boy [or girl] that will be born." That faith is sustained by the exclamation found in I John

3:1–3, which should become a talisman or a guiding reminder for the Christian teacher:

> See what love the Father has given us, that we should be called children of God: and so we are. The reason why the world does not know us is that it did not know him. Beloved, we are God's children now; it does not yet appear what we shall be, but we know that when he appears we shall be like him, for we shall see him as he is. And every one who thus hopes in him purifies himself as he is pure.

Chapter III

THE RIGHTS OF INFANTS

THE FOURTH GOSPEL tells us that "to all who received him, who believed in his name, he gave power to become children of God" (John 1:12). We have discussed already the nature of this "believing" kind of faith to generate personality. Now let us focus on the word "power" used in this Fourth Gospel passage. The title of this book, ON BECOMING CHILDREN OF GOD, comes from this passage. The word "power" here does not refer to an inherent ability but to an authorization, an imparted title for a new status. The word can be translated "right." If so, we would read the passage as follows: "He gave the right to become the children of God" to those who received him and who believed in his name.

Furthermore, the word "become" does not mean merely to begin or to make a beginning but refers to having a family relationship to God. In both the writings of Paul and the Johannine words this family relationship is a gift to be received. The Pauline letters use a metaphor derived from the Roman law of adoption, and the Johannine Scriptures use the Greek symbolism of regeneration, the birth from above.[7] The focus of this chapter will be on the "right" to become children of God. The focus of the next chapter will be on the process of becoming the children of God.

The modern student of psychology must be very careful when he is interpreting the Scripture. Many of the words used in the New Testament are today used in additional and different senses in contemporary psychology. For example, the word "right" in the sense of an inherent ability is not emphasized by

many psychologists when speaking of children. Rather, the
incompleteness, weakness, inability, and helplessness of the
infant is underscored by them. Margaret Ribble says that when
we observe large numbers of newborn babies "we are struck
immediately by their helplessness." They breathe insecurely
and irregularly. They do not adjust to cold easily. They even
need help in establishing the ability to suck and feed. She says
that an infant's nervous system "is incomplete and the brain
is not yet ready to function in control of behavior." She points
to the way in which early painters were a long time learning
that a child does not even "look like a miniature man or
woman." She says that "we ourselves are even more obtuse
when we think of a child's mental and nervous organization
as being like that of an adult but on a small scale."[8]

Yet, on the other hand, psychologists today do refer vigor-
ously to the inalienable rights of every infant coming into the
world. By the very reason that they are infants they have the
right and the privilege of being treated by adults *as infants.*
They are not "little adults." Ribble speaks of the maternal
instinct as a gift of nature that has to do with a child's intention to live, to grow, and to become a completed person.
Mothering, whether it is done by instinct or design, "is as vital
to the child's development as is food." Through this process of
caring the child becomes assured that he is not a thing—"a toy
or an idol"—but an individual who has an innate need for a
loving relationship that is met by the mother. Clues are given
by Holy Writ, as well as by the sensitive insights of Dr. Ribble,
concerning the unformed lives of newborn babies. Therefore,
I would like to use these to identify what I consider to be the
basic rights to which every child that comes into the world has
a privilege. These privileges are his necessities. Adults responsible for him under God are obligated to fulfill these rights.

THE RIGHT TO BE AN INFANT

I recall walking the long wards of a state hospital as a chap-
lain in my early ministry. One day I saw a twenty-two-year-old
woman lying down in the aisle between the long rows of beds,
rolling back and forth and screaming and chattering like a
little child. I came near her, and she noticed my presence.

I spoke to her gently and yet firmly and said, after calling her by her full name: "Tell me, what are you doing?" She replied, "I am being a little baby." I asked again, "What makes you want to be a little baby?" She replied, "They did not let me be a little baby when I was a little baby and now I am catching up on being a little baby." Every infant has a right to be an infant and not to be expected to be an adult. If we do not accord this right to an infant, sooner or later that infant will reach back and claim that right for himself or herself. We cannot put old people's heads on infant's shoulders without grotesque results. This puts the finger of judgment on our unrealistic expectations of infants. We are likely to expect them to feed themselves too soon, keep themselves dry and unsoiled too soon, and think of ourselves as failures as parents when they do not conform to these expectations.

What has been said literally about the growth of infants can be said symbolically about entrée into the Christian life. The Scripture speaks of us as being "babes in Christ," "fed with milk, not solid food." The Scripture both in the example of Jesus and in the exhortation of Paul as teacher takes into consideration the "readiness" of a person for certain teachings. (See I Cor. 3:1–4 and Heb. 5:11 to 6:2.) Admittedly, both of these passages to which reference has just been made are toned with an atmosphere of impatience because people are "past the time" for putting away childish things to whom these two letters are written. Nevertheless, a disclaimer is entered in behalf of the spiritual infant. We are to be mature in all things, but in anger we are to be immature. Milk *is* for infants in Christ. Childlikeness is affirmed as a prerequisite for entrance into the Kingdom of Heaven.

Therefore, both literally and symbolically we can underscore the rights of infants to be infants. The free gift of the children of God is the right to learn the rudiments of experience with Christ in the Christian faith. Here we have a paradox, both sides of which we must live with faith, hope, and love.

THE RIGHT TO BREATHE

The Scripture tells us that "the LORD God formed man of dust from the ground, and breathed into his nostrils the breath of life; and man became a living being" (Gen. 2:7). Dust was animated by the Lord God's *breath,* or "spirit," which made him into a living being, a total self. Primitive man identified life with breathing. As the psalmist says, "When thou takest away their breath, they die and return to their dust." (Ps. 104: 29.) However, breath and spirit are words that are used interchangeably in the Old Testament. The very next words of the psalmist are: "When thou sendest forth thy Spirit, they are created; and thou renewest the face of the ground" (v. 30). Job captures something of the same idea as follows: "The spirit of God has made me, and the breath of the Almighty gives me life." (Job 33:4.)

These words must be very real to the nurse and the doctor who solicitously attend a prematurely born child and watch his every breath. The rhythm of life itself is in the breathing. We await the baby's first cry with hopes realized when this signals that the child is breathing. However, it is wrong to assume that breathing is, therefore, self-regulated and taken for granted. At birth a child must adjust to his new environment and breathe much like an astronaut or a deep-sea diver. Dr. Ribble again tells us that mothering is the important fact that helps to break the deadlock between the plentiful oxygen in the air and the constant struggle of a little child for the physiological sufficiency of breathing. The brain itself takes a lion's share of the developing body's oxygen supply. The lungs must work overtime to meet the rest of the body's needs. Breathing is something that cannot be taught the child. Yet as a child learns to feed himself at the mother's breast, he is helped to breathe by her consistent personal attention. When the child learns to vocalize, even the most meaningless babbling sounds, this is a signal that an inner balance of oxygen through breathing is present. The child's newfound "right to breathe" is established; he vocalizes; delight comes to both mother and child. The anxious child has "shortened breath," and, quaintly enough, one of the Biblical words for "anxiety" means literally "shortened breath." The angry child "holds his breath." Even one of the signs of the depressed child is the sighs of breathing.

Once again we are moving both literally and symbolically to the nature of life itself. Crucial to our day is the right of every living being to unpolluted air to breathe. Radioactive fallout focuses the ethical struggle of mankind today. The pollution of the air we breathe removes the right to breathe and forces destruction that will "return us to dust." Therefore, whether we take the right to breathe literally or symbolically, the results are the same. Especially is this true for little babies.

THE RIGHT TO MOTHERING

The understanding love of a mother is an inalienable right of a child. Mothering is a precondition of becoming a person in one's own right. Mothering focuses in the newborn babe around two great functions: feeding and speaking. Both of these functions involve the mouth. Thus the mouth becomes the nucleus around which the trust and confidence of a newborn child is formed. As a pearl begins with a specific substance, so the personality begins with the mouth. Apart from mothering a person perishes both literally and figuratively. William James used to say that an infant at the outset is a "big, booming, buzzing, confusion." He is not aware of himself as a *self*. His "me" is no different than the rest of the world. He is an undifferentiated self blended into the being of his mother for some time after his birth. Therefore, if he is to become a person in his own right, his mother is an imperative necessity. Her body becomes "the other." Her presence spells security. Her absence spells insecurity.

THE RIGHT TO A FATHER

A young woman, an expert in child care, was lecturing and leading a discussion with a group of theological students about the pastoral care of children. One student asked: "If mothers are so important to the care of a child, what is the place of the father in all of this?" She replied: "The father's best opportunity to care for the child is to make his wife secure in his own love for her. The mother makes the child secure. The father makes the mother secure." The anxious, fearful, bereft mother must have her resources replenished by the strength and admiration, affection and tenderness, wisdom and reassurance of a strong husband. It takes two parents to raise every child. A child has a right to a father who is *there* both to him and to the mother. A Mary can tend her child while shepherds watch in adoration. A Joseph stands between her and unkind neighbors as well as threatening Herods. This Bethlehem scene is recapitulated in every parent-child relationship. The absentee father leaves the infant desolate because the mother is deprived.

The father today, especially in the middle classes, provides much mothering, baby-sitting, caring, and tending in his own right. The taboo on tenderness in men is controverted by the presence of the helpless infant. Yet the protective and providing powers of the father are the focus of his identity as a father. Here he proves himself to be a real man. Can he protect his wife in the time of her preoccupation with and care of an infant? Can he stand by and accept full responsibility for the joys that he had in sexual relationships with the mother of his child? Every child has a right to a father who can do this.

The unchangeable element in sexual ethics can be specified here. The so-called "new moralists" miss the point when they attack Christian ethics for a sex morality confined to marriage and restricted to procreation. Those forms of Christian ethics which restrict themselves to this emphasis also miss the point. We do not hit the mark of sexual ethics until we fix our sights upon the moral principle of a man and a woman *staying by* a helpless child in a unified love that brings a child to maturity. This takes fidelity, communication, responsible love, powers of durable relationship, and plain patience. Child-rearing requires that a man and woman lose their own lives in order that they may save themselves and the child. Here the cross of Christ is implicit in the call to parenthood. The task of the teacher is to enable the parent to accept this as the explicit commitment of the parent. This requires freedom from deception and division of commitment to each other as well as wholehearted dedication to Christ. A child has a right to such parents.

The Right to Be Wanted

All that has been said thus far implies that the husband and wife—father and mother—have *chosen* to be parents of this child. They *wanted* this child. They *agreed* upon having this child. The child has a right to be wanted. He has a right to be brought into the world on purpose and not as the accident of a *Playboy* Philosophy of sex, within or without marriage.

This is the main theme of contemporary education and planned parenthood. A child can be unwanted by unwed parents. The fear of pregnancy is confirmed in the fact of pregnancy. But even more so, a child can be unwanted by wed parents. They may simply not like children. They may have other ambitions. They may already have too many children. They may have had painful and traumatic experiences in previous births. For many reasons they may not want children. Birth control measures are, therefore, ethical obligations of parents in that they widen and deepen the range of choice in becoming parents. We should, therefore, inasmuch as we possibly can, see to it that in prayerful cooperation with God the Creator, every child we bring into the world is wanted. This is the child's inalienable right. *Choosing* to be a parent assures that husband and wife from the very outset have harmonized and synchronized their wishes and long-term commitments in life. It is the precondition of the joy of childbirth and the discipline of parenthood. In this sense, marriage is a creation of God, given to us for the enjoyment of one another and of him in the creative design he has for the world. We can, therefore, partake of marriage with prayer and thanksgiving and thus consecrate our children to him. In doing so we bequeath to the child his basic right to be wanted. This "wanting" is love at its heart. "Love," as Howard Rome says, "is a very light thing." In a new baby's life, "it takes a lot of love to make a pound."[9]

THE RIGHT TO A CHURCH

Every newborn infant is born into the covenant of marriage. The home becomes the center of all the rights of being an infant, of breathing, of mothering, of fathering, and of being wanted. Yet mother, father, and child cannot bear these obligations alone. All together they have the right to a larger family of mankind, which God has designed in the church of the living Christ. Here they have a hundredfold fathers, mothers, brothers, sisters, houses, land, etc., and a promise of eternal life. One "gushes" with an idealism that is out of touch with reality when he assumes that—unaided—the rights that have been mentioned thus far will be accorded every child that comes into the world. Death is in the world too. Sin is in the world too. Death snatches away a mother from the side of a newborn babe. War tears a father away from the side of mother and child. Slavery can shatter the rights of infants. This slavery may be like the slavery of the nineteenth century. Negro fathers were sold away from their wives and children. Industrialization snatched both mother and father—white and black—from the side of the new babe and put them to work in mills. The twentieth-century variety of slavery is just as damaging to the rights of infants though less apparent. Big business can create demands on the organization man in modern suburbia that destroy his relationship to mother and child. Slavery in any garb can shatter the rights of little children.

The intention of God is that the church fill up the empty places left by death, divorce, war, and slavery. The power of God enables the church to transcend destruction of infants' rights by man's inhumanity to man. The Scripture puts it bluntly in one of its rare definitions of religion: "Religion that is pure and undefiled before God and the Father is this: to visit orphans and widows in their affliction, and to keep oneself unstained from the world" (James 1:27).

When I speak of the church here, I am not referring to the vague, nebulous, invisible sort of thing. I am referring to a specific "larger family" to which the family appropriation is "organismically" related. They know each other face-to-face. This larger community supports and sustains the father with inspiration and enthusiasm for his task of providing for and protecting his family. This church leads the father to an independent existence of his own before God and teaches him to pray. This church cheers the father in his discouragement, sustains him in his decisions, and comes to his aid in his helplessness. In the absence of the father, this church fills in the gap left by his separation from his wife and child. It does so without evil design, but with the discipline of unstained hands and uncontaminated motive. In doing so the religion of this church is made pure and undefiled before God.

The pastor of this church symbolizes both the strength of the father and the tenderness of the mother as well as the larger context of the fellowship of believers. He is a shepherd who feeds his flock as a good undershepherd of Jesus Christ. He "attends" unto little children. In the tradition of the Lord Jesus Christ, when divisions threaten the fellowship of the church, he takes unto himself the little children of the church and points to them as the ones who are being caused to stumble. He casts his lot with the little children. This is no sentimental act. It represents the hard-nosed reality of the economy of life as it is. It represents the severity as well as the goodness of God. The infant child partakes of the deposit of faith vicariously through the commitment of father and mother to God in the context of the commitment of the larger family of God, the church. Every infant has a right to such a church. Surrounding him and his older brothers and sisters are teachers like the reader of this book. These teachers bring home to the child his inalienable right in the flesh and blood of their concern and their instruction.

This rather ideal assumption of the right of an infant to the kind of church described here in no wise assumes that no other institutions, groups, and individuals than the institutional church can and do provide this kind of care for persons. I work as a part of the staff of a close-knit psychiatric unit dedicated to the care of acutely disturbed persons. This kind of care and concern appears in the seemingly secular context of this clinic. Sometimes the real community of faith appears as the church and sometimes it appears in other forms. The important thing is that it appear, not that it be haggled over as being sacred or secular.

Chapter IV

BECOMING AN INDIVIDUAL

BASIC TRUST AND FAITH, respected and given rights—these provide the foundations on which an infant rises both literally and figuratively to his feet and becomes an individual. The other of the mother, father, and sibling becomes distinguished from the me, myself, and I. The sense of identity of the familiar figures of mother and father, brother or sister, R. A. Spitz has insisted, precede the sense of being a self in one's own right. He says: "The Thou is earlier than the I." He also says that the awareness of the "I" does not take place until around fifteen months of age.[10]

Allport says that there are three aspects of self-awareness which gradually come to pass during the first three years of life: the sense of bodily self, the sense of a continuing self-identity, and the sense of self-esteem or pride. We can discuss these briefly. The sense of a "bodily me" happens when a child bumps into something "out there" or when he is not permitted to do something he wants to do. It arises further from the exciting discovery by a child that he is more than a "mouth." He discovers a hand, a foot. In turn the hand discovers an ear or some hair.

The bodily sense stays with us throughout life. Alfred Adler said that variations in the organic construction of the body— its size, its color, its handicaps, etc.—provide a "core of behavior" for an individual. One's inferiorities and compensations are established in the bodily sense. For example, a short, a tall, a fat, a too-thin, or a malformed person tends to become a self in terms of these variations. In this day of racial tension, we know that a person's color makes him think of himself as "black like me" or "white like me," etc.

Although the bodily sense is important to one's individuality, it is not the whole of it. As Allport says, "The sense of self depends on more than the bodily me."[11] In the second place, one's individuality continues in his feeling of self-identity. A person who is eighty years old *remembers* himself as also being a person of three. Self-identity is "the accrued confidence that one's ability to maintain an inner sameness and continuity is matched by the sameness and continuity of one's meaning for others."[12]

The child becomes a defined personality within a context of other people who accept him as being the person he understands himself to be. Probably one of the most important aspects of self-identity is one's name, particularly his first name. This is his "given" name. Mankind's confidence in the power of one's name is extremely old. This conviction goes back to the most ancient times, to the most primitive form of intellectual and religious life, and it has extraordinary vitality. The Bible portrays the name as something that is real, a piece of the very nature of the person whom it describes that partakes of his qualities and his power. For example, the New Testament uses the name of God and reveres the name of Jesus as having been given to him as a "name above every name." The naming of a child involves the very dedication of the child to God. It is a "Christian" name. In both infant and adult Baptism, the one baptized becomes a possession of and comes under the protection of the One whose name he bears. He is under the control of the effective power of the name and the one who bears his name, namely Christ. Allport says that "by hearing his name repeatedly the child gradually sees himself as a distinct and recurrent point of reference. The name acquires significance for him in the second year of life. With it comes awareness of independent status in the social group."[13]

In the toddler the sense of selfhood is incomplete but well begun. It may be associated not only with the awareness of his name but also with the ability to walk. About this same time the child learns to walk. He becomes mobile. As he stands up on his "hind legs" and ceases to be a creeper, the child now achieves a keen sense of individuality. Erikson says that parents easily remember skirmishes with children becoming individuals. "He was feeling his oats." "He had a passion to explore." Contradictorily enough, he becomes more dependent and independent at the same time. Parents rearrange the whole house for a wandering baby. They help him to avoid accidents by putting poisons out of reach, teaching him to leave certain things alone, and enabling him to control his aggressive feelings. He learns to bite, kick, throw, and pinch. The muscle system has matured.

When a child begins to exert himself in these ways, we cannot assume that he is an animal that must be broken or a machine that must be set up and tuned. He is an individual in his own right and has joined the war for autonomy. We are in a crisis now with him. He has his "work" to do now. Mrs. Melvin Roberts wrote of her child Mark (one year, four months old):

> Mark's work consists of:
> Sleeping, waking, eating, talking,
> Running, creeping, dancing, walking,
> Pleasing, teasing, loving, cooing,
> Hiding, sliding, and peek-a-booing.
>
> Laughing, singing, smiling, sighing,
> Kicking, tumbling, sometimes crying,
> Hugging, mugging, seeking, finding,
> but mostly Mark's work consists of binding—
> Binding all of us together
> And our hearts to him forever.

This "binding" is the first tender expression of the child's power to *be* an individual before God. Parents walk the narrow ridge between enabling the child to have autonomy and self-confidence as an individual on the one hand and causing him to feel shame and doubt on the other hand. As Erikson has said, "Nobody knows how to fabricate or manage the fabrication of the genuine article" of individuality. However, just as the earliest phase of development is related to faith and trust, this phase in the religious life of the child is related to a sense of law and order in things. Becoming a child of God here means learning to do that which is "becoming," the appropriate thing, the apt thing. This calls for coordination, balance, and direction. Parent and teacher become both inspiration and regulator, a representative of gospel and law.

The fundamental religious problem of teacher and parent here in relationship to the child is establishing a balance between law and grace, restriction and humor. The "all-powerfulness" of the child meets the limitations of teacher and parent. The way in which these limitations are communicated either opens or shuts the door to the grace of God. The law is always a tutor to grace, preceding it with limitation and assuaging it with forgiveness. Here in the fledgling individuality of a child is literally expressed the nature of law and gospel.

The third dimension of individuality is what Allport calls self-esteem. Once a child becomes aware of himself as a self, he has a passion to be himself. He resents "help." This is the time of *"No,* Mother, I would rather do it *myself."* A parent can spoil everything by depriving the child of the opportunity of trying to do something he thinks he can do for himself. A wise and a compassionate pediatric nurse once told me that the main way to spoil a child is to do something for him that he can do for himself or to deprive him of the opportunity of trying to do something for himself that he thinks he can do for himself. This is reminiscent also of the wisdom of the Hebrew rabbi who reinterpreted Prov. 22:6 by free translation of his own. The Revised Standard Version translation says: "Train up a child in the way he should go, and when he is old he will not depart from it." The rabbi gave a free translation of it by saying: "Train up each child in his own particular way and when he is old he will be himself." In other words, *a* child has *the* way *he* should go. The mystique of parenthood and teaching is to discover the uniqueness, the individuality, the very fingerprints of God's intention for a given child.

One way of stating the theological belief that we are created in the image of God is in terms of the self-respect that inheres in an awareness of our own uniqueness as an individual. Here in the self-esteem of a little child are the first tender, green shoots of that awareness. Martin Buber says:

> I . . . apply the name "God" . . . to my Creator, that is,
> the author of my uniqueness, which cannot be derived
> from within the world. . . . The humanly right is ever the
> service of the single person who realizes the right unique-
> ness of purpose for him in his creation. In decision, taking
> the direction thus means: taking the direction toward the
> point of being at which, executing for my part the design
> which I am, I encounter the divine mystery of my created
> uniqueness, the mystery awaiting for me.[14]

We can liken the rights of infancy to the paradise of the
Creation story. We can go one step farther and liken the
necessity for individuality to the temptation story of Gen., ch. 3.
Man walks in the garden in the cool of the day. God chooses to
walk with him, to converse with him, to have fellowship with
him. Yet the bounds of man's habitation are set. The very
awareness of these bounds reminds man of his possibilities. His
curiosity is aroused. He is—whether he be man or woman—
tempted to test these bounds. In his ability to know good and
evil lies his kinship with God. He is caught between the necessity of exercising his free initiative and the possibility of bringing upon himself shame and doubt. He chooses to exercise his
free initiative, and hazards the shame and doubt.

In a little child this same dilemma exists in miniature in
relation to his parents. He becomes aware of his body and runs
the risk of his nakedness and shame. He becomes aware of
himself as a self and cherishes the name given him by his
parents. He becomes aware of his uniqueness and feels the
separation between him and others. At one and the same
moment his individuality is born along with the possibility of
loneliness. The wise parent deals with him with both a firm
representation of reality and a genuine spirit of forgiveness and
love. He can do so because he himself is an individual and
needs forgiveness too.

The parent and the teacher have a priestly role in relation
to the little child in the process of his becoming an individual
in his own right. They are chosen from among men to act on
behalf of the child in relation to God and to offer gifts and
sacrifices for sins. They can deal gently with him in his igno-
rance and waywardness since they themselves are beset with

weakness. Because of their having been beset with weakness themselves they are bound to offer sacrifice for their own sins as well as for those of their child (Heb. 5:1-3).

A MODERN DILEMMA CONCERNING THE SELF

All that has been said here sounds very nice, but it leaves the modern teacher in a real dilemma. Most of our education has been somewhat moralistic about the use of the word "self." The question arises, or should arise, as to what all this means. Have we not from the beginning been taught that the "self" in and of itself is evil? How then can we use the word "self" as if it were a "good" thing? In superficial Christian moralism we tend to think of the body as evil, of ourselves as "a nobody who always will be with no right to live," and self-esteem as self-elevation and evil pride. But in Biblical knowledge, God intended that the whole body of a person be seen as good, that we see ourselves as children of God redeemed by Jesus Christ. He intends that we look upon ourselves as made in his image, as persons for whom Christ died, and as temples of the Holy Spirit. This total self we are to present to God as a spiritual service. This latter interpretation is what I mean by Christian selfhood. Such a perception of ourselves and of little children enables us to teach them to respect their bodies, to know who they are and whose they are, and to have a genuine sense of reverence for themselves as a basis for reverence for others.

When one puts this differently, one could say that a child cannot consecrate a self to God that he has not become. The very act of consecration implies the power of decision and a clarity of one's unique capacities as well as his limitations. We are called upon to inspire this kind of confidence in little children particularly. Otherwise, we cast them into fear and doubt. The reader may well say, though: "Is it not unfortunate that one must talk here about the results of parental conditioning? Are we the victims of fate in having the kinds of parents we have?" This questioning is very important because both teacher and pupil may be in bondage to a fatalism about the kinds of conditioning wrought by parents. Fatalism is not the only way of handling the anxiety about the "curse character" of the past. We can respond to the threat of "not having a self" in the face of the relativities of our personal history by fatalistically surrendering to our previous conditioning. Or, we can respond with hope in the face of the meaninglessness produced by our parental conditioning and appeal our case to a higher authority in God. As Paul Tillich says of his own parental conditioning: "The importance of such parental legacies is not that they determine the course of one's life, but that they define the scope and supply the substance out of which critical decisions are drawn." [15]

> For you did not receive the spirit of slavery to fall back into fear, but you have received the spirit of sonship. When we cry, "Abba! Father!" it is the Spirit himself bearing witness with our spirit that we are children of God, and if children, then heirs, heirs of God and fellow heirs with Christ, provided we suffer with him in order that we may also be glorified with him. (Rom. 8:15–17.)

When we read passages such as this we find no foundation for self-rejection but, rather, Christian paths to self-acceptance.

Chapter V

LEARNING TO COMMUNICATE

BEING AN INDIVIDUAL in one's own right gives birth to the need to communicate with those about us. A child has learned to walk, to stand on his own, to be upright, to look across at his world, to be an individual. Next comes his effort to learn to speak in such a way as to be understood as himself. The miracle of human language very early begins to take place. Responsibility for being an individual produces responsiveness to other individuals. A child becomes more aware of other selves through communication with them.

The simplicity and depth of the Genesis account of the creation of man pictures in vivid symbol the place of language and communication in the unique identity of the human being. The Creation story tells of the infancy of mankind when the Lord God breathed into men the breath of life. It tells of the struggle and temptation of man as he came to stand on his own but in relation to his Creator. It underscores the temptation of man with the powers that were his own in the face of his limitations. The Genesis story also tells of the emergence of language in man's search for companionship. The fledgling "man" "named" the creatures of earth as they were presented to him. Curiously enough the power of verbalization, of putting things into words, grew out of his search for companionship. The Scripture says:

> So out of the ground the LORD God formed every beast
> of the field and every bird of the air, and brought them to
> the man to see what he would call them; and whatever

the man called every living creature, that was its name.
The man gave names to all cattle, and to the birds of the
air, and to every beast of the field; but for the man there
was not found a helper fit for him. So the LORD God
caused a deep sleep to fall upon the man, and while he
slept took one of his ribs and closed up its place with
flesh; and the rib which the LORD God had taken from
the man he made into a woman and brought her to the
man. (Gen. 2:19–22.)

Up to this point language had been a "naming" process. It
was unaccompanied by exclamation or enthusiasm. But when
man discovered woman, he was filled with exclamation and
enthusiasm and said: "This at last is bone of my bones and
flesh of my flesh; she shall be called Woman, because she was
taken out of Man" (Gen. 2:23). In childlike simplicity they
lived together unaware of their own bodies, anatomical differences, and without shame.

Another Biblical story concerning language and communication is found in Gen., ch. 11. It points to the rudimentary
and the simple nature of man in his primitive infancy. The
Scripture says: "Now the whole earth had one language and
few words." (Gen. 11:1.)

But the ambition of man and his desire for communication
with others contradicted each other. Men sought to build a
great tower—the Tower of Babel. Here again temptation to
defy their limitations and to reject that which was impossible
for them raised its ugly head. A confusion occurred similar to
that which occurred between man and woman in Gen., ch. 3.
They were confused in their language and could not understand one another's speech. (See Gen. 11:2–7.) Men were scat-
tered abroad over the face of all the earth, and their languages
were confused.

The Greeks had a wonderful story to explain the struggle
for communication and the ways in which misunderstanding
arises. They pictured Narcissus as being a worldly sort of man,
busy hunting in the fields and woods, running wildly in which-
ever direction he chose to go. He came to a pool of water and in
his thirst stooped down to drink. He saw his own image reflected in the water and fell deeply in love with himself. Self-

love captured him. A girl, named Echo, on the other hand, had a different problem. She was not busy with actions but busy with words. She talked too much. She talked so much that she angered the gods. They chose that only her last two or three words could be heard. That would be enough.

Then, in the remarkable sense of tragedy characteristic of the Greeks, Narcissus and Echo meet each other. She falls desperately in love with him, but he cannot understand her. She talks vainly, hoping to be understood, using much language. But only the last two or three words of what she says can be heard. (So characteristic of husband-wife, parent-child, and child-parent relationships today!) For example, she would say: "I love you dearly, and I want you to love me." All that could be heard was "love me"! He understood her as a brash young woman demanding of him love but offering no love to him. On the other hand, in his own self-love he could not give himself to her. Hence they both languished away in their inability to communicate. Their search for communion with each other was stalemated in their lack of communication.

Biblical Themes
and Modern Insights Into Communication

These Biblical stories and Greek stories have a "faraway" ring to them, but a contemporary melody comes through with rich meaning. Learning to communicate begins early in human life. Freud identified the narcissistic, or self-centered, nature of a young child. The young child has contradictory needs for communion with other people and for self-affirmation. Harry Stack Sullivan went one step farther to say that infancy ends at the time of the appearance of articulate speech. Childhood begins here. Childhood begins when the child develops the ability to utter articulate sounds of or pertaining to speech. Like Adam in the garden, the child learns of that "other world" through his mastery of the "names" of things. He learns to relate himself to other people through the medium of words, however private their meaning, with which he exchanges meanings with them. One of his favorite phrases and questions, babbled out in such unintelligible syllables that only the most

solicitous parent can understand them, is: "What is that?" It
may come out as nothing more than "Zat?" but it *means*:
"What is that?" The response of his parent or teacher is to
"give it a name." That name has been handed down to them
from their parents generation after generation. That name
bears the marks of the family, of the social class to which the
family belongs, of the culture and community in which the
family lives, of the nation of which the community is a part,
and of the language which that "people" speaks.

As an infant, the child received a name. In childhood, the
latter period, he "gives" names. A responsive dialogue or exchange of words is established. As Paul Johnson says: "Every
person is a seeking person. For persons sustain and re-create
each other in the mutual response of community."[16] Language
becomes the medium of this mutual response of people to
each other. Language begins childhood. Language is no mere
biological function of the human being. As Edward Sapir says:

> In a certain sense the individual is predestined to talk,
> but that is due entirely to the circumstance that he is born
> not merely in nature, but in the lap of a society that is
> certain, reasonably certain, to lead him to its traditions.
> Eliminate society and there is every reason to believe that
> he will not learn to walk, if, indeed, he survives at all. But
> it is just as certain that he will never learn to talk, that is,
> to communicate ideas according to the traditional system
> of a particular society.[17]

To be distinctly human is to communicate with words. Nonverbal means of communication are extremely important to
us. Yet, they tend to have their meaning in terms of the
translations we make of them into words. Therefore, this era
of a young person's life is crucial.

THE TONAL QUALITY OF SPEECH

Long before a child can distinguish words or even make
half-meaningful babblings, he is sensitive to tones with which
words are spoken to him. Tones with which he expresses his
sounds represent the tenor of his communication. One physi-

cian tells of observing the amazing instance of an infant whom he saw for the first time. He was amazed that the eleven-month-old infant, in the presence of two adults talking, was "carrying on a very interesting conversation of his own." What caught the physician's attention was "the beautiful tonal pattern." The melody, the pattern of tone, was communicative. It was not verbal, but the child had learned by trial and error, having been raised in a home where speech was spoken correctly and well, "the melodic progression of speech" actualized in the tones of the infant.

At this point the use of music, the singing of words, and the development of rich sounds, tonal patterns, and rhythms "plug into" the baby's private language. The lullaby, the hymn, the communication of religious faith through music— these become some of the earliest ways of creating an atmosphere of care, commitment, and affection around the child. The infant can pick up the emotional frame of reference of the home through the harshness or the gentleness of the tones being spoken around him and spoken to him. These preverbal ways of communication cannot be overestimated in their importance.

In addition to this, an infant talks "baby" talk. If we talk baby talk in return, we may "fix" him into distorted patterns of communication. However, one of the advantages of this baby talk is to communicate the approving and forbidding melodies of speech in the tones.

Learning Words "Fitly Spoken"

A child soon learns three zones of his speech equipment for making tones, sounds, noises, and words. Then he realizes that the lips, the tongue, and the palate provide the labial, lingual, and guttural sounds such as the *m*'s, the *l*'s, and the *g*'s, respectively. A game can be played with the child by taking the *m*'s, *l*'s, and *g*'s, the *p*'s, *t*'s, and *q*'s, etc., and simply playing with the sounds they make. In addition to this, the vowels and the consonants can be played with as the child begins to make music out of his sounds. The parent or the teacher who enjoys playing with children would do well to have some specific games of this kind that fit into his need to learn language.

But language is more than mere sounds. It is a combination of words. Words are names of things and actions. Fingers can be used to point to things. Charades or actions themselves such as run-run-run, sleep-sleep-sleep, etc., become fitted to the right meaning through the use of both the eyes and the ears. Smells, colors, tastes, etc., can be fitted to the right kinds of experience on purpose. At the stage of learning the language, which is dreadfully difficult in and of itself, it is almost cruel to speak baby talk to the child when plain meaning is what is needed. To get the right meaning with right experience knits language and thought together with the people who are important. A student of mine, a young mother of a two-year-old, better than I can say it, described this as follows:

> Dear Dr. Oates,
> I heard Buber's concept discussed in seminary lectures, I read Buber's writings, I gained a superficial understanding of his philosophy, but a few days ago, Mark explained it in terms I could understand.
>
> We were looking out the window of his room, watching the planes circle over Bowman Field when he turned to me, looked me squarely in the eyes and said, "Plane gone, Ma-ma, plane gone." A more direct encounter I have never experienced, for although he had said all of these words previously, there was in this moment of "putting them together" a sense of real communication and suddenly I was transformed from a diaper-changing, food-fixing, toy-picker-upper (IT) to a Ma-ma (THOU) with whom my son wished and could have dialogue.
>
> Prayer—communication with our THOU God—rather than the futile striving after an IT suddenly made more sense.

LANGUAGE AND SOCIAL DEVELOPMENT

As has been said, language is the bridge over which a person goes to community with others. Swiss psychologist, Jean Piaget, has studied the process whereby language becomes the medium of the achievement of social life in the child. He says that children's language can be divided into two large groups—the egocentric and the socialized. The egocentric language takes place when a child utters phrases without bothering to know to whom he is speaking or whether he is being listened to or not. He talks to, for, and with himself. He makes little effort at putting himself in the place or at the point of view of the hearer. He is not particularly concerned with having an audience, because anyone who is there will do. Suffice it to say that this kind of conversation is not restricted to children, but can be heard at any church tea or evening banquet! When the child uses egocentric speech he depends on repetition, prattling the same thing over and over for the sheer pleasure of doing so. He may use monologue, talking to himself aloud and addressing no one. A group of children may have what might be called dual or collective monologue in which a great deal of talking goes on in a group but no one talks *to* anyone or expects anyone to hear. The presence of other children is only the occasion of egocentric speech and not the objective of the speech.

Piaget says a second kind of speech appears as the child matures. This is socialized speech. The child really trades thoughts with others. He tells others things. He listens to what they have to say. He gets information from them. He gives them information. Furthermore, socialized speech is characterized by an exchange of criticism. The child struggles with other selves for superiority and is tempted to depreciate other people. Argument, command, request, and threat resound.[18]

Socialized speech at its heart, however, is composed of questions and answers. Many questions of three-, four-, and five-year-old children are for information and call for answers. Other questions are not for information, but they are asked in order to signal the adult that the child has the answer to the question. Many questions about God, Jesus, creation, evil, death, etc., can be answered simply by asking the child: "Have you worked out an answer to that yourself?" or, "What have you felt about that and what have you come up with as an answer?" This is not to avoid the child's question and should never be used in that way. Rather, it gives the child an opportunity to tell whether or not he wants to convey his answer or to get the answer of the adult. In fact this is a good approach to all questions of people of all ages! There is a certain child-like quality about questions and answers that we never outlive.

Similarly, questions and answers arise with reference to the birth of children, the birth process, the nature and function of the human body, and especially its sexual and excretory parts, and often the child has devised naïve little answers to these questions for himself. Therefore, the parent or the teacher is well advised to explore with the child the meaning of the question, the kinds of answers the child has devised, and to build the adult answer on the basis of conclusions already in the child's mind.

Sex education should begin very early with children. It should begin by teaching the child the right names of the parts of his body. We should not wait until the child reaches puberty or the age of twelve or thirteen before beginning his or her sex instruction. Children become curious about the world, about their own bodies, and about the bodies of their sisters and brothers. Questions and behavior of small children about these matters do not mean to them what the same questions asked by an adult would mean to an adult. They should be answered factually without creating undue anxiety or unnecessary stress.

PRAYER AS COMMUNICATION

Probably the most crucial kind of language that develops in children at this stage is prayer. Here communion between the parent and God should be learned by example. The child can be taught simple prayers. However, these prayers should not become a substitute for the prayers of adults. They often do so in the hurry and scramble of busy households. The father particularly should lead in the experience of prayer and the mother as well. Adults should state their prayers in simple language that can be "picked up" and copied by the child. The beginning of language is the beginning of prayer. The little child comes to know God as a friend, as a great void, or as an enemy, depending upon the atmosphere, the tonal quality, the kinds of words, and the kinds of music he hears at this stage. Lewis Sherrill puts it well when he says that prayer is at the heart of the Christian's experience of God. The parents' and teacher's objective should be to acquaint the young child with our heavenly Father's friendship. Sherrill says that God calls us to turn again home "to be replenished and to rest quietly in the Presence, and to express love in any language of devotion which the soul can use." Prayer, seen this way, is communion with God. Sherrill encourages us to enable the child to share his thoughts with God—his thanking thoughts, his adoring thoughts, his confessing thoughts, and his asking thoughts. He encourages us to listen to God through the words that are given to us by one another. He says that we should stress prayer as a growing friendship and not as a "set pattern for praying." He thinks of prayer as exercising our experience of the presence of God.[19]

Three researchers, Diane Long, David Elkind, and Bernard Spilka, studied the prayer life of 160 elementary school children. They discovered that the concept of prayer appeared to develop in three stages related to age. At the first stage, around the ages five to seven, the child had a *global conception* of prayer, vague and fragmentary. At the second stage, around the ages of seven to nine, prayer was an external activity, considerably routine, ritualized, but it was recognized as a *verbal* activity, one that required words. Yet it was not personal and internal. The abstract conception of prayer as an internal activity expressing personal conviction and belief did not appear until the ages nine to twelve. Only in preadolescence, then, does prayer emerge as an intimate, personal communication between the I of the child and the Thou of God. This will be further in evidence as we discuss preadolescence and the child's need for an intimate friend.

Therefore, the child, prior to entering public school, tends to get more involved in the reality of prayer through the incarnate action of his parents in prayer than otherwise. This underscores the importance of parents' avoiding the common practice of "ditching" the family prayers on the youngest child in the family.[20]

LANGUAGE AND LEARNING THAT WE ARE DIFFERENT

The child soon learns as he moves outside the home that his language and the language of other people are often different. If he comes from the home of uneducated parents, he meets friends who come from the homes of educated parents. If he comes from an ethnic group—Negro, Nisei Japanese, German, etc.—he may discover that his accent is different. His pronunciation of words will be different. While he is outside the home at school, he may learn to speak his native tongue quite differently from the way it is spoken in his home. As a result he may have "two" languages—one for home and one for away from home. If he moves out of his region, he may discover that he is known and identified as a Yankee, a Southerner, as one of the ingroup, or one of the outgroup. Speech identifies him. His identity is tied up with his way of speaking. If he comes from a home where profanity is or is not used, he meets profanity on the playground. As Peter, lisping in his native tongue of Galilee, was identified by his speech, even so are all of us scrutinized in our speech by others to determine "who we are." Therefore, language not only communicates; it *excommunicates*. Language not only creates community; it divides the community. The reason is plain. Language represents the intimate fellowship of those who belong to one another and symbolizes the differences between those who belong and those who do not.

This is the big problem of the church in the world today. We are called upon to be in the world but not of it, to use the language of the world to interpret the gospel to the world. Yet at the same time, we are called upon to keep the words of our mouths and the meditations of our hearts acceptable in the sight of the Lord. Thus in our very speaking we bear the tension of the cross itself. For it was the Lord Jesus Christ who "came to his own home, and his own people received him not." The Lord Jesus Christ was identified as a Nazarene. People asked what good thing could come out of Nazareth. The Lord Jesus Christ himself "suffered outside the gate in order to sanctify the people through his own blood" (Heb. 13:12). In other words, Jesus intensifies to the ultimate extreme the experience of the Christian teacher. We, too, are both accepted and rejected by the world; we live in it but we also live beyond it. We are enjoined to have the wisdom of the world: i.e., the wisdom of the serpents; we are told to have the mind of the Holy Spirit: i.e., to be as harmless as doves. We carry this tension upon us and do not try to be goody-goodies who are not wise to what the world is like; nor do we try to be covert about or ashamed of our identification with Christ.

The teacher who is alert to the language expressed by those whom he teaches will be aware of the way in which speech both reveals and conceals. *What* he teaches creates conflict in the lives of those whom he teaches as well as brings peace to them. He will always be asking: What does my teaching do to change this person I am teaching? What effect do these changes have upon those with whom he associates daily in his home and in his intimate group? Speech will be the conveyor and sustainer of these changes. The "community" embodied in the speech will be the "conversation of life" or "way of life" of both the teacher and the pupil.

Chapter VI

THE HORIZONS
AND THE IMAGE OF THE SELF

ONCE A YOUNG CHILD has become aware of himself as a self, and once he has learned to communicate through language with others, he launches on what Lewis Sherrill rightly calls a "pilgrimage of the self." He begins to extend the horizons of his world and to form clearly a picture of "who he thinks he is." Namelessly, he senses the "beyondness" of life.

EXTENDING THE HORIZONS OF THE SELF

Though a child knows who he is and can communicate through words with others, he is far from a complete self. His horizons are very limited. As with the horizon, it is very difficult for a child to tell where the real world ends and the world of his imagination begins. Even though he can communicate with others and feels a need for a response from them, he will be many years older—even at the age of twelve—before he can understand another person's outlook on life, accept it as one that is as good as his own, and learn to practice empathy with others. He will only with difficulty be able to put himself in another person's place and see the world from his point of view. And, as Allport says, "some adults fail to attain this."[21]

The extension of the horizons of the self comes to pass to a considerable extent through a sharpening of the "sense of the bodily self." The parts of the body, especially sexual parts, increase in their degree of importance and privacy in the mind of the child.

In the years from four to six, the child becomes intensely interested in the bodies of his parents. The little boy by comparison extends himself to the body of his father. The little girl by comparison extends herself to the body of her mother. The normal, healthy, and creative growth of the child requires that the child learn what to do with his body from the parent who has a body like his own. The child adopts the reactions of his parent of the same sex toward persons of the opposite sex. In other words, a little boy, to coin a phrase, "images himself" as a man through becoming like his father. A little girl "images herself" as a woman by becoming like her mother.

If there is a failure in this "imaging" process, the life of the child becomes restricted, his horizons limited, and marked disturbances of his character structure can take place. The parent and the teacher both participate in this. It is not unusual for teachers in church school or in nursery school to have themselves "mistaken" for the parent. They will even be called mother or father. In this stage of the expansion of the self, identification plays a chief role in the formation of the personality of the child. Some of the most momentous changes in the whole life of the person take place at this point and establish the images that guide later behavior. A die, to use a machinist's phrase, is cut here that "influences to some extent later social attitudes, sympathies, and activities, as expressed in political, economic, and religious affiliations and partisanships."[22]

I shall not soon forget a vivid example of this. I visited the dirty, poverty-stricken home of a family in which the father was an acute alcoholic, the mother a prostitute, and the children periodic inmates of a public children's center for neglected and deprived children. At this particular time all the family were together. I was conversing with the father in the front room when a five-year-old boy, the son of the man, came out with a battered, ragged pair of old pants. Nevertheless they were *long* pants. I asked the child, "Tell me, whose pants are those?" He replied, "They are my 'daddy' pants!" I asked him what he meant. He said, "My daddy wears long pants; I wear long pants!" Here a little boy was expanding his world to include the kinds of behavior, the kinds of "identity,"

he had observed in his father. Yet how difficult will it be for
the little boy to express tender affection toward the mother
when there was as much conflict, hostility, and bitterness as I
found between his mother and father.

This expansion of the horizons of the self has been called by
Piaget "the elaboration of the universe" of the child. He speaks
of the world of the child prior to this age as being somewhat
"chaotic." The external world and the self remain disasso-
ciated. An understanding of the relation of objects in space
and time or of cause and effect is not possible. But as the self
begins to "elaborate its universe," time, space, and inner con-
nections between things become better and better differen-
tiated. The constant extension of the lines of "making connec-
tions" between things pushes the thinking of the child "up" to
the new level of reflective thought. He begins to deduce things.
He experiments with different techniques of making connec-
tions, associations, and progressively formed relationships between things, persons, time, and space. In a remarkable way
then, Piaget says: "Intelligence thus begins neither with the
knowledge of the self nor of things as such but with the knowledge of their interaction, and it is by orienting itself simul-
taneously toward the two poles of that interaction that intelligence organizes the world by organizing itself."[23]

Little wonder is it, as we become acquainted with children
who are old enough to begin to play with children outside the
home, and yet not old enough to go to public school, that we
see that they find children's stories such as *Alice in Wonderland*
so very enchanting. This is, as Alice sings, "a world of my
own." The child begins the great struggle between fantasy and
reality which will last for the rest of his life. This struggle is
also basic to religious life. One must have solitude to be
genuinely religious, for as Whitehead has said in a partial defi-
nition, "Religion is what the individual does with his own soli-
tariness."[24] And yet there is a contradictory need in man to
move up and move out of himself and to elaborate his universe.
This calls for communication.

Nicolas Berdyaev, in his essay and autobiography, rightly
says that "withdrawal and communication are acts of human
existence around which revolves the whole religious life of

man."[25] He says that religion aims to provide "an answer" to the question of man's contradictory need for solitude and community by "creating a bridge between two worlds and thus with the realization of kinship and intimacy." Berdyaev was convinced that the experience that he had of himself as a self was one that set him apart from the objective world. He felt uprooted and disestablished in the world. He was on the defensive against the world and kept watch over his freedom. He let his very sense of loneliness and estrangement, although it made him "an absentee even when he was actively present in life," nevertheless cause him to be actively committed to life and to those around him. The disharmony between him as a self and the nonself around him brought him pain and disquiet. This pain and disquiet caused him to be allured by and drawn toward the transcendent, the Other which reaches out beyond all boundaries and limitations and holds within itself the mystery of life.[26] This impelling sense of need to expand the horizons of himself gave Berdyaev "from childhood . . . a strong sense of vocation."

As we look into the life of the Lord Jesus Christ, we discover him coming to terms with such limitations of human existence. Therefore, teachers must examine the meaning of the expanding horizons and the image of the self in terms of the Biblical perspective of this very important phase of religious life. The phase begins just prior to entry into nursery school and kindergarten, continuous through that time as a psychological beginning. As a major spiritual issue it continues throughout life. The Biblical wisdom on this subject, imperative as it is, is the next topic.

THE IMAGE OF GOD AND THE SELF-IMAGE OF MAN

In I Cor. 11:7, Paul tells us that man is "the image and glory of God." Here he relies precisely on the Old Testament understanding of the image of God. The image of God in the Old Testament "means personality, provided we remember that this must not be understood in the sense of the autonomous, self-legislating self" apart from God. Man is determined by God as his creator. By "image of God" may be meant what gives authority, and that God has made man to exercise such may imply responsibility.[27]

But the New Testament conception transforms the idea of the image of God from this to that found in Rom. 1:23. There it seems to mean something similar to "likeness" and to imply a complete correspondence or perfect representation of an original image. As in Heb. 10:1, the perfect likeness causes all other imperfect likenesses to cast shadows. However, God is the "Father of lights with whom there is no variation or shadow due to change" (James 1:17). Christ is the image of God. Heb. 1:3 says: "He reflects the glory of God and bears the very stamp of his nature." In Col. 1:15, Christ is "the image of the invisible God," and in II Cor. 4:4, Christ is "the likeness of God." In Christ man can attain the likeness to God which at first was promised him in creation. Becoming a Christian means expanding the horizon of one's self-image to identify with the living Christ. Paul speaks of this as being "crucified with Christ" and "nevertheless living" (Gal. 2:20). This identification with Christ means exchanging the old self for a new self "which is being renewed in knowledge after the image of its creator" (Col. 3:10). This comes to pass through the transforming power of love and infinite devotion. It is energized by a spiritual communion in which "we all, with unveiled face, beholding the glory of the Lord, are being changed into his likeness from one degree of glory to another; for this comes from the Lord who is the Spirit" (II Cor. 3:18; compare Phil. 3:20–21).

This can all be brought down to earth and to the children with whom we work and live. The process of the "elaboration of the universe," which Piaget has described, and the process of identification in the parent-child relationship described by a psychoanalyst all are dynamically akin to the experience of worship. The parent-child relationship is a worshipful one. The child, particularly when he is expanding the horizons of himself and defining his self-image, finds in his parents and teachers those "shadows" which stand between him and the Father of Lights in whom there is neither shadow nor turning. Refraction and distortion occur. The child gets a glimpse of the light of the Father in heaven through his parents and older persons around him, but he tends to see them as his "gods." His God is anthropomorphic—by which we mean he thinks of God in terms of people. The people are those who are most important to him—his parents in particular. He takes into himself their likeness. They are the undershepherds of Jesus Christ. Insofar as Christ dwells in them and is adequately conveyed to the child by them, the child participates in "the deposit of faith" that is in them. This intimate bond of the creative love of God between parent and child overcomes the loneliness of the child. At the same time, his individuality is not destroyed. The community need of the child is met without demanding servility and conformity. Freedom and responsibility are brought into dialogue through love.

Hazards of Idolatry

The intimate bond between parent and child can easily be turned into a shackle of idolatry. The parent can worship the child and thereby constrict the elaboration of the child's universe. He can do this by causing the child to feel real guilt when he exercises initiative. The parent can clamp down on the child's image of himself as he comes to that crisis, "more or less beset with fumbling and fear" when

> the child suddenly seems to "grow together" both in his person and his body. He appears "more himself," more loving, relaxed and brighter in his judgment, more activated and activating. He is in free possession of a surplus of energy which permits him to forget failures quickly and to approach what seems desirable [to him] (even if it also seems uncertain and even dangerous) with undiminished and more accurate direction.[28]

The child begins to demonstrate the characteristics necessary to plan and attack a task, exercises self-will, even shows acts of defiance, and certainly desires independence.

On the other hand, the child may feel guilty about being himself. He may transform this guilt into a mimicry, an imitation, a compulsive need to please the parent. He may be immobilized until he can get the clue and cue to go ahead from his parents. Thus the parent, in demanding conformity and creating guilt about initiative, gets in return idolatry and overdependence. From a strictly theological point of view the *skia* or the "shadow" mentioned in Heb. 10:1 obscures "the likeness" of the image of God appearing in the individuality and initiative of the child himself. Thus idolatry becomes the groundwork for interpersonal incompetence, an off-centered life, and a self-image that is askew from reality.

Such a responsibility placed on the parent is staggering. However, the wisdom of parents quite often is enriched by the native gumption that comes to them as they follow their feelings rather than the things they read. The purpose of describing the enormity of this task is not to increase but to identify the responsibility of the parent. A parent himself can profit by seeing the tension and anxiety created by these idolatrous restrictions on the child. He can relax his demand for a reflection of his own perfect likeness in his child. He discovers a more relaxed and happier relationship to the child. In other words, joy takes the place of anxiety, optimism takes the place of fear, and fellow human participation takes the place of the tyrant-subject relationship between parent and child.

The most poignant thing that can happen to a child's self-image, however, is emotional starvation, i.e., to have neither mother nor father with whom to identify. Such was the plight of children in World War II in the blitzkrieg of London. Anna Freud tells of gathering a little child up in her arms and asking him his name. He told her that he didn't know his name. He told her that he guessed he was "nobody's nothing." This deprivation of the self-image causing a child to feel that he is "nothing" and is "nobody's" is devastating. The Scripture centers the Christian faith just at this point. We are to be children of God, heirs of his by adoption, and joint heirs with Jesus Christ. We who were "nobodies" are to be somebodies in Christ. This is our image. This is who we are. The intention of God is that we see ourselves as we really are. This means that our self-image is that of a person created in the image of God. Our self-image is that of a person for whom Christ died. Our image of ourselves is that of persons who participate in celebration and joy in the family of God where Jesus Christ is our elder brother, God is our heavenly Father, and the Holy

Spirit is the lifeblood that energizes and nourishes the life of the church. The deprivations of our earthly heritage are prevented from destroying us by the communion of Christians.

THE TEACHER, THE CHURCH, AND THE EXPANDING SELF-IMAGE

The family cannot bear the burden of the care of the child alone. The child needs more than father and mother with whom to expand his world and build an adequate self-image. The responsibility of parenthood crushes when borne in isolation. The fellowship of the church provides a larger family of mankind in which parenthood becomes a boon and not a bane, a fellowship and not a lonely struggle. This is particularly true when illness makes one or the other or both parents inadequate, when war separates the members of a family, when divorce makes a one-parent family of one or the other partner, and when death takes one or both parents.

I associate with this truth the vivid memory of the plane accident death of both mother and father of a young ten-year-old boy. For some yet unknown reason, the plane went down in the Pacific Ocean. The whole church gathered quite spontaneously with the grandparents and the lone child for prayer as search missions sent one dismal report of failure after another. Since then, different members of the church have filled in the gaps left by this awful tragedy. They have mitigated the grief. They have become images of loyalty and fidelity for the growing boy.

If you have read the story of the slide of the coal slag pile in Aberfan, Wales, as it crashed into the school building wiping out the majority of the children in the town, you will ask: What does this do to the remaining preschoolers as they think of entering school? What sort of image has been imprinted upon them by the remaining believers in Christ? Suffering has bound them together. What quality of binding is it? The church can heavily affect that quality.

Or, take the son of an alcoholic whose father is periodically incapacitated by the disease of alcoholism. Are there adequate persons who can, during these times, support and sustain the emotional need of a child for an adequate person with whom he can identify and like whom he can safely become? Or, must he form his *whole* image of the masculine side of the human race from this one sick man, his alcoholic father?

These are tragic dimensions of the need of children for adequate persons who serve as working models in their building and expanding their image of themselves. More subtle, however, are the needs of the young child in the home where the parents are conscientious, adequate, and even very, very adequate and successful. Why is it, we ask, that children from such parents and homes are often among the underachievers, do not have much ambition, and seem not to turn out as well, measured by conventional norms of success? Let me hazard a guess.

Teachers, pastors, neighbors, and even relatives move on the assumption that the children of successful Americans will *naturally* turn out likewise. They assume that these children do not *need* anyone other than their families. Yet, they need someone outside their home in a different way from the bereaved child, the child of an alcoholic, etc. They need a person other than their own family members who will care for them for their own sakes. They, too, need a steadfast friend, teacher, and guide. Their adequate parents can never do one certain thing for them: they cannot be a faithful friend *on the outside of the home* who will accept them as an individual *apart from* their parents. The successful parent cannot hide his or her success from his or her own child. The very success itself might intimidate, overshadow, and discourage the child. This might give him a feeling of fear to try anything on his own lest *he* fail. As a result he does not try.

The child's alternative, even at a very early age, is to "get out" where he *can* grow. He may develop a vastly different set of interests from that of his father. His individual way of doing things stands in bold contrast to that of his parents. He adventures in expanding his self and creating and maintaining his own self-image. If his parents feel rejected and reject him in return, the child of the privileged family more desperately than ever needs the teacher and the church. The teacher must know him, see him as a person becoming the child of God and not just as the son or daughter of such and such a big wheel in the community.

Therefore, the teacher of preschoolers, elementary-age children, and especially high school young persons should be strongly advised to care less about the position of importance of the parents of a child from an affluent home. They should give careful individual attention to the child for his own sake and his own sake alone. The *first* name of these young persons means more to them than their last names. They may not like to be reminded of their parents' status. They prefer to be themselves. For example, one preschooler would not go to the country club to swim. She wanted to go to the Y.W.C.A. Her mother would try to deliver her to the Y.W.C.A. in a latest model Cadillac. She would not permit her mother to do so. She got out of the car two blocks away and walked the rest of the way in order not to be seen in a Cadillac!

The teachers and leaders of such a child who assume that all her needs for people outside the home are met by her parents are badly mistaken. She is deprived in a subtle and strange way. The church that is sensitive to this will discover the new meaning of the church to the affluent. It is with their children! Here they live as parents in quiet despair. Their children have the material goods of life and hunger for someone to take up some time with them for their own sakes alone. Underneath it all, they may have a low self-image—fearful of failure, passively hostile, and desperately misunderstood.

THE SELF-IMAGE AND RELIGIOUS PURPOSE

Aspiration is born into consciousness at or about the time the child is in kindergarten, from four to five years of age. The image that a child has of himself becomes the guiding light of his life. As an individual, he is like the Children of Israel in search of a promised land. His self-image is a pillar of fire by night and a cloud by day. As Erikson says, "Unbroken initiative for a high and yet realistic sense of ambition and independence" is borne here. Yet he could just as likely be laden with guilt here. He is not only ashamed when found out but afraid of being found out. As Erikson again says, "He now hears, as it were, God's voice without seeing God."[29] The value of life and of religion most precious at this stage is *purpose*. The vague stirrings of the "calling" of God and of life begin here. The sense of sin here is not over what one *does,* but over *not having* done what one could have done. It is the remorse of missed opportunity.

Communication with the child, then, about "right and wrong" is clearest when the teacher learns to participate in the dreams and imaginations of the child. The child is beset on every side by frustration. He knows few, if any, adults who are at heart childlike themselves, filled with the "joy of desiring," the playfulness of the never-never world—even though they do have a sturdy sense of the demands of the real world. In short, the teacher must demonstrate a sense of poetry and art in working with the kindergarten age. Art forms, game forms, song forms, story forms, and the world of nature itself provide the channel of communion with the child "as he sees himself from within himself."

Here the teacher has an opportunity to learn from the child. He or she will experience bursts of truth and insight coming from what the child says of himself. The child will tell of his present abilities, place in the world, and the "part" he plays in the drama of the life of his family and the play and work group. He will confide his aspirations, his *purposes,* what he is "gonna do" and "gonna be." He buffers these against the teacher, and this should bring out the "grain" of his being without scarring the surface of his self-image.

If the teacher sees himself aright, the very character of God's revelation of himself *through* the child comes through to the teacher in this openness of eye and ear to what the child is saying and doing. The schoolteacher in the Broadway musical was right when she said that if a person becomes a teacher, by his or her pupils he or she will be taught.[30]

Probably, however, a living documentary of a young mother's description in her own words says more precisely what is meant. As a teacher and parent she learned *from* her child as he began to expand his horizons and as his self-image became the directing pattern of his life. These parents, as wise parents do, introduced new people to their four-year-old by having them as guests in the home. These were friends from overseas—one Nigerian-African, the other Japanese:

David Idowu (Nigerian) and Isao Nabekura (Japanese) were visiting with us the other evening. Both men have families many miles away and our son "took" to them wholeheartedly. He was fascinated by Isao's Japanese sandals and played the game of leading Isao to the door to put his shoes on, then take them off. David said something about bananas growing so large in his country (Mark was eating one at the time) and Mark associated David with "banana good" and led him to his room to show him something. They made four trips to see whatever it was. The spirit of fellowship we enjoyed that evening was kindled and brightened by Mark's spontaneous acceptance of his two new friends. David remarked of the pertinence of Christ's statement, "A little child shall lead them." (Believe those are Isaiah's words, but Christ reinforced them!) Once again we were overwhelmed with the wonder of having a little one to teach, to help grow, and from whom to learn and "be helped to grow" ourselves.

The self-image of a child forms around the estimates those near to him have of him. It also grows in terms of the *comparisons* they make of him with other persons like whom they wish he would become and *unlike* him whom they fear he will become. The church school teacher has the opportunity to expand the horizons of the child's self-image here. He becomes acquainted with people of different socioeconomic and cultural "places" in life. The suburban teacher of well-to-do middle-class people can acquaint the child with inner-city deprived persons. The down-and-out mission child can meet the teen-age youth leader from an affluent neighborhood. A group of children in a charity hospital can meet a group of high school young persons as teachers and visitors on Sunday morning. The "bored" teen-ager in a suburban church can go to a Negro church where the worship patterns are different.

Race prejudice and social class snobbery and inferiority have their beginnings in the early years just prior to entry into public school. The child builds these into his self-concept as his horizons are limited and not expanded. The lyrics of the *South Pacific* song are right when they say that social class and racial hate are not born in us, but that it happens after we are born. We have to be taught to hate. Others "drum it into our little ear" before we are seven or eight. We have to be taught to hate the people our relatives hate.[31]

The Christian gospel speaks to these restrictions of the self-image of a person with Paul's firm injunction that "from now on . . . we regard no one from a human point of view" (II Cor. 5:16). The point of view we have of ourselves and others is plain: We are made in the image of God. We are *persons* for whom Christ died. We are of one blood with all mankind.

To fix these "images of the self" in even a little child is the task of the teacher—that "Christ be formed in them." This lowers the importance of the distortions of the image of Christ inherent in every human relationship. This safely moors the aspirations and the behavior of a child without our becoming his policeman. This gives him access to the larger family of mankind. Through loving identification with the wise and patient teacher, the child begins that long pull toward maturity put into a few words by Jeremiah:

> But this is the covenant which I will make with the house of Israel after those days, says the LORD: I will put my law within them, and I will write it upon their hearts; and I will be their God, and they shall be my people. And no longer shall each man teach his neighbor and each his brother, saying, "Know the LORD," for they shall all know me, from the least of them to the greatest, says the LORD; for I will forgive their iniquity, and I will remember their sin no more. (Jer. 31: 33–34.)

Chapter VII

ON MEETING TEACHERS
AND SCHOOLMATES

THE SIX-YEAR-OLD CHILD is young, has a measure of experience with playmates, and yet is placed on the edge of entering a whole new world: school. He is a fully functioning self, though an inexperienced self. He has come through four stages in the organization of his personality. Erik Erikson says that the first stage has crystallized around the conviction: "I am what I am given." This is the stage of helplessness, of infancy. The second stage is one in which the self forms around the conviction: "I am what I will." This is the stage of individuality. The third stage of the expansion and clarification of the self-image may be characterized by the conviction: "I am what I can imagine I will be." Here the child works at distinguishing fantasy from reality. The fourth stage marks the child's entering school. Then the personality of the child crystallizes around the conviction: "I am what I learn." As Erikson says, "The child now wants to be shown how to get busy with something and how to be busy with others."[32]

At school the child meets other children. They are potentially competitive or cooperative beings. He also meets teachers. He is now to receive systematic instruction. Teachers are to "give it to him." But it is not as simple as that. He has more than one set of teachers. He has the classroom teacher who teaches literacy and does so by appointment, for pay, and in the structured situation of the classroom. However, there are other teachers—the mechanic at the garage, the clerk in the hardware store, the salesperson in the record shop, the librarian

in the library or on the bookmobile, the old retired man down
the street who has time to play with children and to teach them
how to make things, and a dozen other such people. Even more
than this, the child learns on the grapevine between him and
other children. They teach him the ropes. These, too, are
sources of learning. The formal, appointed teacher who is
unaware of these less formal tributaries of learning simply
passes his pupils in a darkness of his own making.

GREAT HAPPENINGS AT SCHOOL

Two great happenings take place when a child goes to
school. First he moves away from the personal kind of authority
of his parents to the impersonal: principal and teachers. On
the way to school he sees an impersonal authority: the crossing
policeman. In the classroom he sees the schoolteacher. On the
playground he meets the recreational director. These people
lay down rules and regulations, many times not interpreting
their meaning to him. It is not his to ask why; it is his to do or
die.

In addition to these adult authorities, there are those people
who, Harry Stack Sullivan says, are "in almost every social
situation: malevolent juveniles—bullies."[33]

These authorities form an imposing complex to which the
child must learn to relate himself. His relationships may be
complicated by the character of his parents' relationship to the
larger community. In a large university town, the child of the
university professor is immediately tagged. In a large political
center such as the state capital or the national capital, the
politician-father's name stamps the child. Furthermore, the
color of his skin, the background of his parents, the cost of his
clothes, and the nature of his speech tend to "pigeonhole" him.

The second great change in the life of the child is the breathtaking shifts that must take place in comparison with the way
in which the child has lived at home. Sullivan calls this second
change "social accommodation." The home presents, even in
its grossest form, the kind of refinement in interpersonal relations that the school rarely provides. A crudeness that is almost
never displayed in later life is the order of the day. Learning

how to cope with bullies, how to maneuver oneself in relation to people who have come from vastly different kinds of homes, how to accept or reject the estimates that one's peers have of one—all these and a thousand other such instances provide an intensive part of the educative process. The healthy child comes to school with freedom to compare himself and his parents with other children and their parents, the teachers, etc. The unhealthy one is the compulsively bound child who looks upon all authority persons as being perfect, as persons whose words are never wrong, and as persons who are to be slavishly followed without asking questions for guidance and clarification.

In the midst of these changes, competition, cooperation, and compromise become the bases upon which the young school-child copes with the world around him. Learning to perform successfully in the period from the first to the sixth grade calls for "industry" and "production" as the child learns to talk, to read, and to act properly in the presence of a crowd of people not his own kin. He experiences himself as a self, but he shapes his life in such a way that his self becomes a sharpened instrument for coping with the reality of the world of which he is a part outside his home. Gordon Allport calls this the development of the self as a "rational coping agent." In this process of the development of the self as a rational coping agent several things happen that are of primary religious significance.

RELIGIOUS ISSUES IN THE SCHOOL COMMUNITY

The religious issues in a school community are far more subtle than whether or not the teacher reads the Bible and prays or whether or not the Supreme Court of the United States thinks this is constitutional. The fundamental religious issues are far more acute, subtle, and difficult to identify. Yet their importance is so great as to make even the Supreme Court seem irrelevant.

The first religious issue is the way in which children, in their early school years particularly, *stereotype* one another. Stereotypes are simple classifications of people, necessary as a "short-hand" way of communicating. For example, we say that the lady at the desk who types is a "secretary." But this does not make all secretaries a segregated society with invariable characteristics. This is classification, not stereotyping.

For another example, in my early school years I was a child who could not afford to bring money to school to buy my lunch. I very soon saw that there were two groups of people who tended to stereotype each other—although I did not know that word at that time. I did feel stamped. I brought a sack lunch. Certain other children did not. Harry Stack Sullivan says that in his own early years he heard many things said about Jews but did not know any Jews. His whole knowledge of Jews arose from studying the Bible. He rejoiced that he did not fix in his mind some of the grimier characteristics of Jews which other children around him had in their minds. Therefore, he was freed of the bondage of stereotypes of "Jews." To the contrary, he had an intense curiosity to find out "what the devil the people who wrote the Old Testament must have been like."[34] A young woman says that when she went to grammar school she had never heard of the idea of thinking literally of a Negro. She did not stereotype them as being a fixed class of people as a result. Now she worries about her younger sister and brothers because they are going to school in a community where race prejudice against Negroes runs very high.

Teachers can aid and abet this stereotyping process. In doing so they restrict the growing child's access to the largest family of mankind. They can make patronizing remarks about miners' children in the consolidated school or in the local church. They can pick "teacher's pets," or they can slant their sympathies toward the girls and away from the boys, a very common habit of women teachers.

The church school teacher, therefore, is well advised to be aware of the stereotyping process that goes on, not only in the weekday school, but in the church school as well. When the church school teacher says that in Christ there is neither male nor female, bond nor free, Jew nor Gentile, etc., the teacher has real data from the public school system with which to work in illustrating this fundamentally religious value.

A second religiously important problem arising in the public school era of the early years of the school life of the child is the relationship between his hearing and doing. The Scripture tells us that we are to "be doers of the word, and not hearers only." Much of the formal educational process is concentrated on some supervisory person talking while some supervised person listens. This is likely to turn the most diligent listener into a spectator, or a leader into a listener. Therefore, the classroom can become a prison by reducing the person's impulse to act because of the sheer oversatiation with words. Furthermore, his consciousness may be constricted in that he uses only his ears with which to learn. His other senses are not involved. But the great sacramental systems have an element of education that has been dropped out of our literacy type of education, with its heavy emphasis on words and its loss of the use of other senses than the ears. The use of incense appeals to the sense of smell. The use of the rosary appeals to the sense of touch. The use of artwork appeals to the sense of color in sight. The use of kneeling, standing, and processing and recessing utilizes the sense of touch and the exercise of muscles.

One of the most creative places in which to implement all these many rich senses of the child in learning—thereby avoiding the constriction of consciousness to hearing—is in the vacation church school. Here processions, pageants, audio-visual aids, group participation in worship, arts and crafts, etc., are implemented. Much of the narrowing of consciousness that later on requires expansion through the use of psychoanalytic free association, sodium amytal, interviews, hypnosis, perception-expanding drugs, etc., may well have begun at the level of the earliest schooling of young people through the constriction of consciousness to unnecessarily verbal methods of teaching. The advent of television forms of education, audio-visual techniques of learning, language laboratories, and direct experience of field activity offer opportunities to avoid such constriction.

The experience of prayer itself calls for a widening of the consciousness of children and adults. Worship, especially through the use of the Sacraments or ordinances, provides a rich and abiding method of opening the range of attention and experience of elementary-age schoolchildren. The Eastern Orthodox practices include even the smallest child in the Holy

Communion. This indicates a wisdom on their part from which Western Protestants could learn much, whether we adopt the particular ritual or not.

A third religiously significant experience of elementary-age children is the development of their attitudes toward their own social judgments and social handicaps. The ethical consciousness of a child as to his own worth and the worth of those around him has its most rapid growth in this era. The child who is sick at intervals and whose illness removes him from school, recurrently preventing him from taking part in physical activities, will tend to see himself as socially handicapped. The child of the town drunk (or the children of the town drunks, more accurately) may be so branded as to be "edited out" of the normal relationships of his school group. The rural child who comes to a large city to school may be nicknamed a hick. This is a day of high social mobility of parents and children. Being uprooted because of his parents' military, business, and other considerations disrupts the life of the child in his juvenile society. He becomes "the new kid" in a juvenile group.

All of this speaks to basic religious values that can be taught by the church school teacher, as well as the weekday school-teacher. For example, the sense of alienation begins here. A person is an utter stranger. He feels his complete separateness from others. The Scripture advises us to be careful how we entertain strangers because we may be entertaining angels unawares. In the very experience of the differences of race, custom, language, social class, community reputation, organic inferiorities, we may teach children—if indeed we have learned it ourselves—to see people not as strangers but as consummately interesting persons in whom we may discover fresh knowledge of God. When we see someone quite different from us, we first experience him as an intruding stranger. But the ingroup that is wholesome and ventilated will reach out toward the image of the stranger. They will form *new* ties. In doing so they enlarge their own world and their own understanding of God. They become more secure as selves in their own right. Here we have a new view of spiritual growth. One becomes orientated in living, not just integrated as a self. The fear of others—especially those who are different—is cast out by those with courage endued by love. Perfect love casts out fear. By perfect love we mean plainly to reach out beyond one's ingroup and to affirm those who are different.

Christian education calls for such extension of the horizons of the self through a careful rejection of stereotypes, an avoidance of passive substitution of listening for participating in life, and the removal of exclusiveness from the child's world view. The end result of the learning process avoids the malignant growth of the capacity to disparage others. Disparagement is commonly thought of as snobbishness. Thus education is not education at all. It is merely the casting of artificial pearls at real swine! The nonconformist student is thought of as inferior, as not fitting in. In return, his parents feel threatened, and the teacher is disparaged as well. This process of disparagement, Sullivan says, "strikes at the very roots of that which is essentially human—the utterly vital role of interpersonal relations."[35]

THE CRISIS OF SCHOOL LIFE

Parents smite their breasts and feel totally responsible for the difficulties in living experienced by their children. Such feelings were more appropriate in the era of the nineteenth century when America was predominantly rural, when the family was more a working, learning, and affectionate unit than it is today. The parent, even by law, must share the responsibility for the education and rearing of his child with the public school. The parent, by the impact of massive religious institutions, is caused to feel guilty if he does not share the religious upbringing of his child with the church. Therefore, school, church, and home cooperation sum up the shared responsibility that all three have in our complex society for the way a child turns out.

The crisis a child experiences upon entering school is a drawn issue between his sense of industry in producing things and bringing a particular job to completion on the one hand and his sense of inadequacy and inferiority in not producing things and not bringing a particular job to completion in such

a way as to please his teachers. The teachers become the judges
of both the parent and the child. The teachers become the ones
who hand out the "goodies" of approval or the "bitter fruits"
of disapproval. Both the child and his parents participate in
the "goodies" and the "bitters." As Erikson says: "Family life
may not have prepared . . . [the child] for school life, or school
life may fail to sustain the promises of earlier stages in that
nothing that he has learned to do well already seems to count
one bit to the teacher."[36] Erikson notes how exciting it is to
observe in the lives of gifted and inspired people "that one
teacher, somewhere, was able to kindle the flame of hidden
talent." In one of his letters, Thomas Wolfe describes how his
relationship with one teacher brought forth the "great music"
that was in him.

To Margaret Roberts

Harvard Club
New York
Monday—May 30, 1927

Dear Mrs. Roberts:
. . . You say that no one *outside* my family loves me more
than Margaret Roberts. Let me rather say the exact
truth:—that no one *inside* my family loves me as much,
and only one other person, I think, in all the world loves
me as much. My book is full of ugliness and terrible pain
—and I think moments of a great and soaring beauty.
In it (will you forgive me?) I have told the story of one
of the most beautiful people I have ever known as it
touched on my own life. I am calling that person
Margaret Leonard. I was without a home—a vagabond
since I was seven—with two roofs and no home. I moved
inward on that house of death and tumult from room to
little room, as the boarders came with their dollar a day,
and their constant rocking on the porch. My overloaded
heart was bursting with its packed weight of loneliness
and terror; I was strangling, without speech, without
articulation, in my own secretions—groping like a blind
sea-thing with no eyes and a thousand feelers toward
light, toward life, toward beauty and order, out of that
hell of chaos, greed, and cheap ugliness—and then I
found you, when else I should have died, you mother of

my spirit who fed me with light. Do you think that I have forgotten? Do you think I ever will? You are entombed in my flesh, you are in the pulses of my blood, the thought of you makes a great music in me—and before I come to death, I shall use the last thrust of my talent—whatever it is—to put your beauty into words.[37]

Just as easily can one find from conversations with students ways in which feelings of inferiority have been bound upon them by teachers. The child is called upon to master the complexities of a technological society. He must have know-how. But more than that, he must have a relationship in which a teacher believes in him when he has trouble believing in himself. One man speaks of his own mother as his teacher: "Mother took for granted that I could do anything the other children could do and made me believe it. Her insight and confidence in me made a lifelong difference."[38] The effective teacher works at the base of motivation that is trust formation in the student. He assumes that his students are there to learn until as individuals they prove otherwise. He does not assume that they will not work unless he makes them move like quarry slaves under the threat of external anxiety.

It is easy to find the teacher who is tyrannical and impatient with a lack of productivity and has a prissy affection for those who conform in every detail to his or her wishes. Therefore, I think it important to conclude this chapter with a careful study of the relationship between teaching and the individual's maintenance of integrity and faith in himself and others.

TEACHING, SELF-CONFIDENCE, AND THE INTEGRITY OF THE INDIVIDUAL

The teacher of today deals with his class members in the context of the intimidating complexities of a technological society. The person can be replaced and misplaced in such a society. So can the teacher. The teacher addresses himself to the person amid these complexities. His class members come from a wide spectrum of varied communities. As individuals they are usually unaware of the complexity of the society in which they live. The alert and informed teacher must be aware of these complexities. Yet this creates a communication gap between him and his students.

The teacher in the church classroom is concerned with the preparation of suitable growing conditions for the emergence of self-confidence and integrity as Christians in those whom he teaches. As a teacher, I find it to be a problem of balance to get across the communication gap between my students and myself. At one and the same time I am called to develop my students' individual integrity as persons and to maintain my own. From the difficult work of being a teacher myself, I would like to suggest a few clues for constructive thinking about the integrity of the individual in the teaching relationship. When I say "constructive thinking" I mean just that. I could join that group of professional mourners in the teaching profession or I could join that group of professional cheerleaders in the teaching profession. But I prefer to face the task of teaching and counseling individuals toward integrity by being neither a joiner, a mourner, nor a cheerleader. You and I are interested in the beams and bolts that hold children and youth together when they are under stress in a technological society. A creative combination of optimism and pessimism presents the Christian alternative of hope. Hope transcends the present circumstance and sees beyond it. With this realistic hope in mind, let me suggest four clues for both maintaining and creating the integrity of the individual in the teaching relationship.

Clue I: The teacher who hopes to contribute to the integrity of the individuals whom he teaches is captured by a conviction that what he says and does makes a difference between life and death for some whom he teaches. This is not true of all the people whom he teaches, but it is true of some.

Here we draw a distinction between learning as retention of data and the transmission of information on the one hand and learning as an event in living on the other hand. The teacher must dare to see his teaching as making a difference between life and death for some of those whom he teaches. He is not nearly so interested in the student's remembering everything that he as a teacher says as he is interested in causing something to happen in the life of the person that he cannot forget.

Anton Boisen often said that the teacher and counselor work with three different groups of persons all the time. The first group is that group of creative persons who will thrive and grow regardless of what the teacher does. The second group is composed of those persons who are so resistive, concealed from themselves, and satisfied with themselves that they drift and surrender regardless of what the teacher does. The third group is that group to whom the teacher makes the difference between living and dying, between hope and hopelessness, between purpose and purposelessness. The effective teacher is always searching for this third group. He does not ignore, lose hope, or neglect the other two groups, but he searches for the third group.

In this sense the teacher is what Holden Caulfield in J. D. Salinger's novel spoke of as a "catcher in the rye." The teacher sees himself caught up in the game of life with crowds of young children around him. He is aware of the cliffs at the edge of the abyss and sees teaching as "coming out from somewhere" to catch people on "the edge of the crazy cliffs" of life. This feeling of necessity may seem unbelievable to many people, but a real teacher understands it.

Clue II: The teacher or writer contributes to the integrity of the individual when he sees him as a total person, as "a body" in the Old English sense of the word. Incidentally, this is the Pauline use of the word "body" too. It refers to the total person.

Seeing the student as a total person is a difficult thing to do in a technological society that has been fragmented as has ours. The average youth in school has to integrate too many roles—many of them conflicting with one another—into one person. Maintaining consistency and integrity and taking into consideration our students' many-faceted roles in life is a major issue in the student-teacher relationship.

When we look at this from the point of view of the student, we see him as a member of two families—the family into which he was born and the family which he is yet to form when he marries. We see the student, furthermore, as a member of many "joining" groups. The elementary or high school student of today is not only in church groups but in social clubs, high school classes, and extracurricular activities in his high school. In turn, he or she may be a member of other groups to which his or her parents belong. Integrating these roles, scheduling them into the dimension of time, and maintaining conflicting loyalties present a task that can tear an individual asunder. The sensitive teacher is aware of these conflicting roles. He sees his teaching as an attempt to help the individual to maintain integrity amid the conflictual demands laid upon him. This calls for coaching in the decision-making process and companionship in the heavy stresses of life.

The teaching relationship, therefore, on the part of both the student and the teacher can in effect become a process in which we learn how to keep from becoming phonies with each other. The multiple personalities of today are tragic witness to the organism's attempt to live, at different times, in terms of different sets of values and different roles. The purpose of education is to bring order out of this chaos, integrity out of this confusion, and harmony out of dissonant demands.

Clue III: The teacher of today who is concerned with the integrity of the individual is sensitive to the problems of discontinuity—i.e., the creation of something new—and the problems of continuity—i.e., the conservation of what is good but old in the process of learning. In Biblical terms, the good scribe brings things both new and old out of his good treasure. Much education consists of amputating the past rather than evaluating, assessing, and threshing the past for what is good. In order to maintain integrity a child must have some degree of respect and confidence in his home origins. In order to have integrity, on the other hand, a person must have some degree of freedom from his past in order that he may continue to grow and lay hold of that which is new. In the words of Robert Frost, he must have something he can look back upon with pride and something he can look forward to with hope. Erik Erikson's formula for identity is helpful here. Identity and integrity are developed through a double process—a clear sense of continuity in which we are "the same" yesterday, today, and tomorrow. At the same time we are something different from that which we have ever been each day we live and grow. The purpose of teaching is to maintain this double perspective of the individual's integrity.

Clue IV: The teacher who is concerned with the integrity of the individual recognizes and seeks to overcome the student's distrust of and mixed feelings toward authority.

Working thinly under the surface of the minds of many of those whom we teach is that conception of a world as a jungle of inconsistency. Thus the child considers himself a stranger to the world. He holds out against it as an alien from the commonwealth of mankind. He holds himself back from such an inconsistent world in noncommitment.

This noncommitment is characterized by a taboo on loving impulses, inasmuch as they are seen as signs of weakness. This noncommitment is a smoldering cauldron of mixed feelings of love and hate toward people of strength and commitment. The uncommitted person suffers a radical split between confident loyalty on the one hand and trustful affection on the other hand. This split expresses itself in a beatnik negative identity of manipulation. They "plug in" into the commitment of others. But they distrustfully hold themselves back from any commitment to anyone. Such a student baits the authority person or the teacher into being punitive and then accuses him of injustice. He is double-minded, indecisive. He loses courage when confronted with the necessity for decision and choice of identity. He has the demand for production "thrown at him" in such a way that he freezes in inaction; feelings of inability "clobber" him with anxiety.

The teacher of today must come to grips with this distrust and fear of inconsistency within himself before God. It is not just a problem of the student. The jaundice of noncommitment is rather readily apparent among teachers themselves. Once the teacher has come to grips with this double-mindedness, distrust, proud inferiority, and ambivalence toward authority within himself, he comes face to face with what Paul Tillich has called the problem of love, power, and justice. Then he can move with some degree of clarity as he seeks to produce integrity of commitment in his students. In both the teacher and the student, that which we withhold makes us weak. As Frost again says, and until we find out that it is ourselves that we are withholding, we do not discover the integrity that the teaching-learning situation has to offer both the teacher and the student. Once we discover this, we find "salvation in surrender." We stand with our students at the gates of a new life in the fullness of a consciousness that we both are and are becoming children of God.

Chapter VIII

PREADOLESCENCE:
THE JONATHAN AND DAVID STAGE

WE LEARN in I Sam. 18:1,3 that "the soul of Jonathan was knit to the soul of David, and Jonathan loved him as his own soul. . . . Jonathan made a covenant with David, because he loved him as his own soul." Jonathan was abundantly unselfish with David as he shared his robe, his armor, and even his sword and bow and girdle with him.

I am not at all sure how old Jonathan and David were at this point. However, I am sure that this is a vivid description of what happens to a young boy or a young girl in preadolescence. Preadolescence has been neglected in our overemphasis on "teen-agers." In the process of perceiving, behaving, and becoming children of God this is an acutely important era. Harry Stack Sullivan has called this the "chumship" era.

A new type of interest appears somewhere along about the age of eight and a half and continues up through twelve to thirteen. This new type of interest is in a particular member of the same sex. This particular friend becomes all-important. You can notice it clearly. Ask a young person in this age group who his or her closest friend is. I recall visiting in a strange home once. An eleven-year-old boy was introduced to me. I greeted him and asked him to tell me who his closest friend was. He blurted his name and dashed out of the room and in a few moments was back with his friend to introduce him to me! Here genuine love of brother to brother or sister to sister *outside* the family circle is experienced. As Sullivan says: "The other fellow takes on a perfectly novel relationship with the person concerned: He becomes of practically equal importance

in all fields of value." A very important capacity is being developed here: the capacity for real sensitivity to what matters
to another person. And as Sullivan says again, "The emphasis
is not a selfish one—on what one can get for himself as to what
he wants. Instead it is an unselfish one as to 'What can I do to
contribute to the happiness or to support the prestige and
feeling of worthwhileness of my chum.' "[39]

COLLABORATION VERSUS COOPERATION

In the earlier phases of grammar school the patterns of
cooperation and competition are predominant in the life of
the growing young person. In the juvenile era of grammar
school there is a rough-and-tumble learning of the give-and-
take of the playground. Black eyes are given and received, and
a pattern of cooperation is worked out before the sun goes
down. Industry is stimulated by competition. The small fry
become little capitalists! They learn to need one another in
terms of what they can get out of one another and do for one
another. The juvenile era is a time when compromises are
worked out in such a way that "everyone wins in a contest of
kindness."

In this competitive, cooperative, compromising era, God is
looked upon as one who "does things for us." God is loved not
for himself but as a matter of one's own best interest. Of
course one does not have to be a grammar school child to have
this attitude toward God. Many persons never get beyond it.
This is the basis of prudential ethics—we love and serve God
because this is the wise thing to do; to do otherwise is to "plow
ourselves under"; to do otherwise is stupid. The smart man
serves God. He serves God for his own sake and not for the
sake of God himself.

But in the chumship era of which Sullivan speaks things are
different. Cooperation, competition, and compromise are not
the order of the day. Collaboration is. Sullivan says:

Collaboration . . . is a great step forward from cooperation—*I* play according to the rules of the game, to pre-
serve *my* prestige and feeling of superiority and merit.
When we collaborate, it is a matter of *we*.[40]

A public school teacher or a church school teacher is not "my" teacher but "our" teacher. It is the real emergence of the "we consciousness" in human life. Here a "child" of God crosses over and becomes one of the "children" of God. An older and much less well-known psychologist, Fritz Kunkel, moves on the assumption that from the beginning of life the human being participates in what he called the "original We-experience." Yet through the encounter with self-centered adults, the We-experience is inevitably shattered and must be restored. More recent psychologists underscore the importance of preadolescence as the time of the restoration of the We-experience in collaboration of young persons with another individual of relatively their same age and sex. Learning to collaborate rather than to cooperate is its core. Learning to collaborate rather than to compete against one's peers—as a form of learning—has several characteristics that identify this "we" experience.

CHARACTERISTICS OF THE "WE-EXPERIENCE"

The first characteristic of the love that is formed between two "chums" is *intimacy*. Intimacy means closeness. Closeness is experienced without fear. One cannot experience closeness to a chum without at the same time learning its opposite—distance. Distance from other people is felt by comparison with the intimacy one feels to one's chum.

A second characteristic of the preadolescent's collaboration with his chum is *comparing notes*. These young people talk with each other confidingly. They "try out" their ideas, feelings, experiences, etc., in conversation with each other. Each component of life is validated or invalidated in this process of learning from each other.

A third characteristic of this collaboration is *equidistant warmth*. Persons of the same sex learn how to be close to each other without becoming erotically involved with each other. Parents may become extremely anxious about the secrets, the whisperings, the gigglings, and the overabsorption of these young people of the same sex with each other. Parents who themselves have had painful scrapes with homosexual behavior earlier in their life or who are insecure about their own sexual identity will tend to project their own feelings upon this chumship. They misinterpret the behavior as being "bad." However, what is really happening is an inoculation against this kind of promiscuous homosexual behavior later. It has been my clinical observation in counseling that persons who are plagued with homosexual fears, homosexual episodes, homosexual behavior, or become confirmed in homosexuality as a way of life—all of which are different—tend to have missed this normal homophilic stage of their typical growing-up years. Ease, competence, and security in working with persons of one's own sex tend to be built upon having been fortunate enough to have entered into and profited from a chumship in the preadolescence phase of personality development.[41] Therefore, the work adjustment of the later adult tends to be built upon the kinds of collaborative abilities that are developed in this era of life.

Furthermore, another characteristic of this collaborative era of life is *secrecy*. Little wonder is it that children of this age are greatly intrigued with mystery stories, cloak-and-dagger adventures, and hideouts. They will build secret places under the steps that lead to the basement, have hideouts in old barns, build tree houses from which to "spy" on the world, and carry on engrossingly private conversations with one another. Two young girls can be seen walking through subdivision streets intensely involved in conversation. Two young boys can be seen astraddle their parked bicycles talking back and forth with each other endlessly. Boys or girls can walk into the house after having just come from one or the other's homes and immediately pick up the telephone and begin a long conversation by telephone. Younger children who listen in are clobbered for snooping.

One of the most important things that is happening in these "secret" sessions is a vital form of sex education. A good measure of verbal invective is hurled at the opposite sex, much teasing goes on, and persons of the opposite sex are loudly protested to be "awful." However, the sexes eye and watch each other. The chums talk to each other about the opposite sex. They confide in each other their "secret passions" for a certain little girl or a certain little boy. In effect, preadolescence is a "launching pad" for later adventure into fellowship with the opposite sex. It is an excruciatingly sweet and painful experience at the same time for a preadolescent boy or girl to take initiative toward a person of the opposite sex. As they move toward adolescence, however, they can do so "in twos" with more security, safety, and freedom. Two boys riding bicycles can stop for a chat with two girls walking or riding much more comfortably than one boy could talk with one girl. In fact, at this age, the latter would probably not happen at all!

Both public school teachers and church school teachers should be aware, therefore, that sex education in its rudimentary form is propitious at this age level. Twosomes of chums could be invited to come together to discussion groups by simply suggesting to members of groups that they bring their best friends with them. Information becomes to them like choice morsels to squirrels. They grab the information, go off together, and talk about it and digest it with each other. Furthermore, efforts on the parts of parents and teachers to push preadolescents into cross-sex social behavior such as dances, junior cotillions, etc., are absurd. They are not immoral by any manner of means. They are just stupid. They represent the needs of adults more than they do the needs of the young people. Large-group swimming parties, hayrides, weekend retreats, etc., are much more effective.

THE RELIGIOUS PERCEPTION
OF PREADOLESCENT BOYS AND GIRLS

The years from nine to twelve are often years of quickened religious consciousness. The preadolescent begins to develop the capacity for intimacy, and the experience of personal prayer can be nurtured as a tender and intimate friendship with God. The words of the hymn by James G. Small speak pointedly to this need for intimacy:

> I've found a Friend; oh, such a Friend!
>   He loved me ere I knew Him;
> He drew me with the cords of love,
>   And thus He bound me to Him;
> And round my heart still closely twine
>   Those ties which nought can sever,
> For I am His, and He is mine,
>   Forever and forever.

I've found a Friend; oh, such a Friend!
He bled, He died to save me;
And not alone the gift of life,
But His own self He gave me.
Nought that I have my own I call,
I hold it for the Giver;
My heart, my strength, my life, my all,
Are His, and His forever.

This kind of emotion a preadolescent boy or girl tends to feel toward his or her chum. Regrettably the Biblical story does not tell us about the kinds of friends our Lord Jesus Christ had when he was on his way up to and back from the Temple. He went into the Temple and sat "among the teachers, listening to them and asking them questions." We do not know with what other young people he talked on his way up to the Temple or what went on between him and his friends as they finally found their way back down to Nazareth. However, we do know that he later had the capacity in an unhindered way to express his affection for his disciples and to build around him a collaborative companionship of persons his own age. The very character of the church which he established was built on their capacity to be open with one another, to be loyal to one another, and to express affection for one another.

The wise teacher or the parent "beams in" on the close friendships of young people with one another. He or she takes them seriously but does not pry into them too closely. Yet he or she creates an atmosphere of acceptance and trust in which these friendships can grow. Thus the foundations are laid for effective churchmanship later. The parents or teachers are nurturing the capacities for intimacy, confident confidentiality, trust, and admiration. They are bringing the cross of Jesus Christ to a level of simplicity that is not "too bright or too good" for the simple need of a young preadolescent boy or girl for a close friend.

Religious decisions are often made by preadolescent boys and girls. Churches of the Great Awakening such as Baptist, Methodist, Disciples, etc., have traditions of evangelistic meetings in which decisions for Christ are made. This age group of preadolescents is often pushed rather stringently to make individual decisions for Christ in evangelistic meetings. Presbyterians of some parts of the country are themselves not exempt from this kind of tradition. However, unrealism on the part of adults doing the pushing causes them to miss the chumship character of the decision-making processes of preadolescents. As Jesus sent out the seventy, two by two, preadolescents have a way of making decisions on a two-by-two basis! Just as moving toward the opposite sex is a threatening experience all by oneself, even so moving toward the church is a terrifying experience for the preadolescent. As one preadolescent child told me: "I love Jesus. He's my friend. I believe in God. He created the heaven and earth. But all that mumbo jumbo about gettin' baptized gives me the willies." "Seduction of the innocent" by "hucksters of the gospel" drives the compulsive adult to grab these young persons "while they can be reached." Therefore, much exploitation of them misses the real opportunity for religious nurture, namely the nurture of their capacity for intimacy with another child their own age and sex, the nurture of their interpretation of God as a friend "who loves them ere they knew him," and the provision of the "inside information" that a child needs to mull over as he or she contemplates "the secrets" of God.

Furthermore, worship can mean much to a preadolescent boy or girl, particularly when art forms, music, and poetry are used to communicate the infinite mystery of God, to communicate the unbounded expanses of the galaxies of the universe, and yet at the same time, in the person of the Lord Jesus Christ, to introduce God to the preadolescent as his "intimate friend." Such communication of the gospel will be heard by a preadolescent. A response should not be forced; it should be allowed to come spontaneously. If it comes spontaneously, one can almost predict that its spontaneity will arise out of one of the twosome friendships that have been formed on the playground, at school, in the neighborhood, and in church school.

SPIRITUAL DAMAGES IN THE CHUMSHIP ERA

Several things can happen to damage the spiritual life of a preadolescent boy or girl. First, parents may develop forbidding behavior toward the chumships formed by the boy or girl. A young person may choose a friend from a different social class. The friend is not judged on the basis of his merit as a person or on individual worth. Instead the parent judges the chum in terms of the kind of neighborhood, the side of the tracks, or the kind of work his parents do, or other superficialities that mean more to prestige-conscious adults than they do to preadolescent boys and girls.

Mary Chase writes an enchanting play called *Mrs. McThing*. Mrs. McThing had a young son about the age of which we are speaking here. She was wealthy. She even insisted that the dentist bring his dental chair to the home to look after the child's teeth! She did not permit the child to go to school. He had a tutor. She would not permit him to have playmates, and said to him that she felt that there was nobody like him, that other children did not have that special something that he had.[42] She thought that buying him an Alaskan dog and having a chemical company to freeze a lake so that he could go dog-sledding in the summer would substitute for a close friend and a chum. But the unraveling of the play came when she, by the strange alchemy of love, arrived at the point she could permit him to have friends of his own choosing. He told her that before she did this he used to think that she was "two-thirds jerk, even if she was his mother." But after this, he said he was proud of her and asked her if she would do him the favor of shaking his hand!

A second spiritual damage that comes to a child in preadolescence is bereavement at the loss of his chum. Sometimes this happens because of the death of a chum, but this is rare as compared with the loss of a chum by the uprooting of the family from one neighborhood to another, from one city to another, etc. Some time ago I read a news account of how an eleven-year-old boy and his family moved from Roanoke, Virginia, to another town 150 miles away. The moving truck was packed carefully. When it arrived at its destination at the eleven-year-old's new home, much to everyone's consternation the chum of the eleven-year-old boy had "stowed away" on the underpinnings of the trailer truck and ridden all the way to be with his chum! Another nine-year-old boy was deeply bereaved when he moved from one side of a large city to the other. In the rearrangement of the furniture of their house, he said to his father that he felt that a separate little room should be set aside as a room for prayer. The father asked him how he had come to think this. He explained his grief over his separation from his friend and said: "We need a room in which to pray at times like these!"

It is inevitable that such moves must be made. One way of overcoming their damaging effects is to arrange periodic visits back to the old neighborhood, exchanges of visits on the part of the child with his chum, etc. However, many parents move from place to place quite unaware of the importance of these close friendships to their preadolescent boy or girl.

One of the most vivid expressions of the importance of intimacy, the collaboration, and the validation of experience that occurs in preadolescent chumships came to me and to my wife as we listened to a twelve-year-old girl who had just moved into our neighborhood from a distant city. She explained how difficult it was to get accustomed to her new school, although the teachers were kind to her. She said she felt very alone there. I asked her if she had a friend back at her other home who meant a lot to her. She began to describe her friend. She said:

> Yes. I sure have! She's the kind of person that I could talk to. Ordinarily it is a rude thing to talk about yourself, how you feel, what things are like to you, and to say the things that you can't say to anyone else. But it was never rude to talk this way to her. Even when I couldn't say how I felt, she seemed somehow or other to know already how I felt and sometimes could tell me what I was feeling. She could talk and talk and talk and talk to me, too; I liked to hear her talk about herself. That's what being a real friend is. It means knowing that somebody likes you more than they do themselves. It means having somebody you like more than you do yourself.

How could I say it better? This exquisitely articulate young girl had learned how to put her feelings into words by having a friend who was willing to listen rather than to talk and in listening to feel that she had talked.

THE CHALLENGE OF TENDERNESS AND COMMITMENT

I began this chapter with a discussion of Jonathan and David whose souls were knit together in love. Yet the challenge of their tenderness and commitment to each other has a strange "farawayness" for contemporary adults who rear and teach young people. As these words are written wars are raging in the Middle East and the Far East. As American people, we are coming to see ourselves as the policemen of the world. We follow the model of *pax Romana*, a country with power ruling the world with legionnaires who "enforce" peace. We present a strange conglomeration of a world to preadolescent boys and their future girlfriends. Consequently, as Margaret Mead has called it, we live in a world in which there is a "taboo on tenderness." A man is thought weak if he is kind and gentle. A girl outwardly bids for a "strong, silent" man, but inwardly cries out for a gentle, articulate man. Such is our poignant mixture!

Even in the days of Jonathan and David, this was true. They expressed their love to each other by sharing shields, bows, and arrows. Jonathan gave his armor to David. Sadly enough, men could not wage war if they did not love one another. Their tenderness for and commitment to each other makes them "buddies" even in the foxhole or the battleship gun turret.

But the preadolescent chumship era sets the example for the kind of tenderness and commitment of which Christian adulthood should be made and with which it should be characterized. This is tenderness in strength. In our Anglo-Saxon taboo on such emotions, we wait until times of great grief, calamity, and terror before these emotions come to surface. Yevgeny Yevtushenko, the Russian poet, published a volume of poems in Moscow in late 1966 entitled *Mail Boat*. In it he has a poem called "Tenderness," which speaks to the condition of which I am now thinking with you as my reader. Intimacy and collaboration of preadolescent boys and girls does not wait to give a "modicum of tenderness" at some crucial time such as death. When they are at their best—and this group of young people usually are—they commit themselves to one another in tenderness and steadfast devotion. They do not pronounce tender speeches for the benefit of history. They express their devotion in acts of affection. Adults of all ages can learn from them.

Chapter IX

EARLY ADOLESCENCE:
AN AGE OF LONGING AND LIMITATION

THE AGE OF THIRTEEN has a sort of magic in the mind of the young person. The thirteen-year-older has joined the teen-ager's society. In primitive cultures an individual goes directly from childhood into adulthood. A South Sea island tribe will have puberty rites. Sometimes even the child's name is changed so that there will be no doubt that he is no longer a child. In the Jewish religious ceremony of Bar Mitzvah, as a young boy comes to the end of his thirteenth year he is ceremonially removed from his seat among the women as a child. He is placed in the midst of the men as an adult. His prayer cap and his shawl represent religious maturity. He is referred to as "Mr." But, as Robert A. Blebs says:

> The only difficulty here is that religious maturity repre-
> sented by the Synagogue is separate and distinct from the
> social maturity represented by the culture in which the
> boy lives. The transition is made easier for him, however,
> by his family's recognition of his new status even though
> it will have to be proved many times over to his Gentile
> contemporaries.[43]

Protestant religious groups have little or nothing in the way of "rites of passage" to recognize the emerging adulthood of the thirteen-year-old. Subtle things of an almost nonverbal nature happen, however. For example, as Arnold Gesell says, both boys and girls "may withdraw from close confidential relationship with their parents." It is a "pulling away."[44] A boy may tell his father that he does not like to have him put his arm around him. Or he may just pull away from him when he does. The family in response may shift its ways of expressing affection. For example, the father may begin teaching the thirteen-year-older how to hunt and to use a gun. The mother may talk "woman talk" with a thirteen-year-old seeking her advice on clothes, jewelry, hairdos, makeup, etc. The whole family may cease to call a thirteen-year-older by his or her "baby" name. A little girl called "Wootsie" will now take her formal given name, Marcia. Adolescence has begun! But at the verbal level and the ceremonial level, everybody becomes inarticulate and insecure as to "what to say and what to do." This wordlessness and insecurity can be relieved by some plain talk as to what adolescence really is in our culture.

WHAT IS ADOLESCENCE?

Complex urban culture with its child labor laws has created a gap when a thirteen- to eighteen-year-old boy or girl is too old to do the things that children do and not old enough to do the things that adults do. This leaves them in the middle. The farm child, even today, has an advantage in that even from early childhood he can participate as a part of the working unit of the family on the farm. Not so with the urban child in an industrial and technological society. Furthermore, the business, industry, and professions of our day require long periods of education even past high school. At or about the age of thirteen the boy and girl "ripen" physiologically. They are capable of producing an offspring. But the social world in which they live is not ready for them to do so nor are they. Therefore, adolescence can be defined culturally as a gap between childhood and adulthood. During this time people expect the young person to hold his or her newfound biological growth under severe control and to meet the heavy expectations of adulthood by getting more education, etc. Thus longing and limitation collide.

Seen positively, therefore, adolescence is a training ground for adulthood in a complex society. It is literally "boot camp" for adulthood. The adolescent is thrown into a crisis of courage and adventure. He longs for adulthood and collides with the limitations of the community about him. Hence I have called early adolescence particularly an age of longing and limitation.

The crisis of adolescence is intensified in smaller families. Here parents heap their needs for a little child to cuddle upon the emerging young adult who is "too big to be cuddled." Furthermore, the crisis of adolescence is intensified when parents and community do not devise ways of encouraging the young person toward adulthood and of providing "support and supply" as a "home base" to which the young person can return from his "forays" and "patrols" into the adult world.

Several figures of speech can be used to describe the function of the church and school in the lives of adolescents. Both church and school are "bridges" over which the adolescent may go into adulthood from childhood. Church and school are bridges to the home as an island and to "the larger family of mankind" as the mainland. Teachers and pastors are arbiters of the best interests of the child, the family, and the culture. They are secondary institutions of society which have been put here in order to lower gradually the importance of the family, give the emerging young adult—the adolescent—more psychic space and "breathing room," a gentler control over his aggressive and sexual impulses, and a wholesome access to the larger family of mankind.

Another figure of speech to describe the church and the school as a function in the life of the adolescent is that of a telephone exchange. They are nerve centers of communciation. It is their responsibility to "plug in" the individual home with the rest of the community. This calls for something more than just a hit-and-miss communication system. The job of the church and the school is not to create a ghetto of neat and managed perfections. Their task is to put the fearful but energy-laden child into the larger community of mankind with values and a sense of direction that will sustain him from within.

A third figure of speech that describes the school and the church in the life of the adolescent could be drawn from the military: they should provide "basic training" for the conflicts and sacrifices required on the battlefield of life. They should take the person on "maneuvers" that will flex unused muscles and bring all faculties to full strength.

Rarely do we give Sigmund Freud credit for having a positive idea of the place of religion in the development of the human person. In one of his case histories, speaking quite apart from his customary concern with pathological problems, he spoke of the positive objectives which religion should seek to achieve in the education of the individual. He said:

> It [religion] puts a restraint upon the child's sexual tendencies by affording them a sublimation and a safe mooring. It lowers the importance of his family relationships, and thus protects him from the threat of isolation by giving him access to the great community of mankind. The untamed and fear-ridden child becomes a social, well behaved adult amenable to education.[45]

In this statement we see a clear outline of the psychological functions of religion in adolescence: Religion provides ethical guidelines for the emotional demands of the growing individual. It provides companionship as the adolescent becomes lonely in his search for autonomy from his home. It introduces him to the whole community of mankind, regardless of race, creed, or color. Religion gives him courage as he copes with his own wild emotions and brings them into discipline without dissipation. By no means are these emotions merely the specifically sexual ones. The aggressive-hostile feelings are just as important. Furthermore, the tender emotions of kindness and altruism tend, according to some authorities, to be buried even more deeply, bringing this great symphony of feelings to the crescendos and heights of maturity. This is the challenge at the door of the church and school.

The home needs its symbolic representation too. In simpler cultures the work, the marital partner, the place of dwelling, and the problems of leadership and "followship" are somewhat settled by the tribal organization. But in the dynamic open society of a complex world of industry, business, profession, military service, etc., the adolescent does not have these things decided for him, nor are they decided overnight. These call for adventure, experimentation, trial and error, training maneuvers, and lonely personal decision. As Charles Stewart says, the adolescent must cope creatively with the adult and peer challenges before him. "Openness to the novel, to the creative, and to the recreative forces of life, to mystery—the very stuff of religion—enable the adolescent to become who he really is."[46] If we see adolescents this way, then we can see them as adventurers and adventuresses. They move out of the home. Literally, as a jet plane leaps into the air with full thrust, they experience the excitement and the risk of adventure into new and untried experiences. Yet the jet must be guided by air traffic control from the ground, and it also must have a "place to land"—to be serviced, refueled, and its crew refreshed.

The home is literally "a landing strip" to an adolescent. There is much landing and taking off. The adolescent comes in with adventures to report, new gains to boast of, and setbacks to bemoan. He is wounded in his adventures occasionally. Sooner or later he always gets sleepy and usually is hungry. A continuing need is "debriefing." The parent and/or the teacher must be open and listen for "the signs" of "what happened." When he does this, the teacher or the parent learns and through the process of listening and minimal interpretation he can teach. A group of adolescents described their teacher as follows. (This can be a guiding image for both teacher and parent.) They said, speaking through one of their more articulate members:

> Our teacher is an older person who is really interested in us. He became a part of us instead of expecting us to become a part of him. He felt he could understand us better if he came into our world instead of expecting us to come over into his world. It was easier for him to come down to us than it was for us to come up to him. He had plenty of time for us. We could feel at ease and not embarrassed when telling him something. He was trustful and pretty honest about the things he said and the way he talked and the way he went about things. He showed us that he really cared about the teaching he was doing. He put his heart and soul into what he was doing and was not slipshod about his work. He was understanding when we were not able to come up with what he asked for. He did not pop off when we did not do as he wanted us to do. He put up with those who didn't cooperate.

Such a "debriefing" approach to the adventures of adolescents is the function of the home; it *can* be a function of the school. Often the school—either the public school or the church school—must perform this function because the home itself is defunct for one reason or another. Let us now look at the processes and atmosphere of early adolescence.

WHY *Early* ADOLESCENCE?

I have divided adolescence into early adolescence and late adolescence for several reasons.

The first reason is that bodily changes take place in the early years of adolescence on a major scale. In girls, there is a general filling out of the "hollow places" and at the same time an apparent rounding out as well. Most girls have menstruated before their fourteenth birthday, and Gesell tells us that "the average thirteen-year-old has achieved ninety-five percent of her mature height." In boys there is a rapid growth of the genitalia, appearance of pubic and axillary hair, a deepening of the voice, etc. This is not true in all thirteen-year-olds but in most of them. Gesell tells us that by the beginning of the thirteenth year most boys have started their sudden spurt of growth in height, and by the end of the thirteenth year "just about half of the boys will have reached their peak rates of growth, and thereafter they will grow more and more slowly."[47]

These bodily changes affect the self-image of the early adolescent. Their appearance concerns them. The mirror becomes a magnet to them. They become more definitely interested in their clothes and personal grooming. The mirror of the external bodily image is matched on a symbolic level by an intense awareness of their inner self. Gesell and his associates tell us that "inwardizing awareness" is a cardinal maturity trait of early adolescent development. This, on the other hand, is linked and interlocked with "externalizing awareness." An exquisite autobiography of an early adolescent is found in the diary of Anne Frank. Hear her as she describes what Gesell has just identified.

> I saw my face in the mirror and it looks quite different. My eyes look so clear and deep, my cheeks are pink— which they haven't been for weeks—my mouth is much

softer; I look as if I am happy, and yet there is something
so sad in my expression and my smile slips away from my
lips as soon as it has come. I am not happy, because I
might know that Peter's [her secret boyfriend] thoughts
are not with me, and yet I feel his wonderful eyes upon
me and his soft, cool cheek against mine. . . . Once when
we spoke about sex, Daddy told me that I couldn't possibly understand belonging yet; I always knew that I did
understand it, and now I understand it fully.[48]

The longing for communication and collaboration with the
opposite sex begins in early adolescence. This is another reason for emphasizing early adolescence. The beginning of this
longing is important. First adventures, however shyly and inwardly taken, in maneuvers toward the opposite sex have a
stamping effect on later experiences. The bodily image and its
awakening longing is again expressed by Anne Frank:

I believe that it's spring within me, I feel that spring is
awakening. I feel it in my whole body and soul. It is an
effort to behave normally, I feel utterly confused, don't
know what to write, what to read, what to do. I only
know that I am longing . . . !

MEANINGFUL RELATIONSHIP TO GOD

A second reason why I emphasize early adolescence is that
the capacity for reaching out to the universe as a whole and
being consciously, voluntarily, and intentionally related to
God is possible now. Gordon Allport says that "to feel oneself
meaningfully linked to the whole of Being is not possible
before puberty."[49] Religious faith—which is more than just
passive assent to verbal statements about religion—is a part of
the great longing of the early adolescent. However vaguely
defined it is or may be, the early adolescent demonstrates the
self-critical and self-improving individual "whose passion for
integrity and for a meaningful relationship to the whole of
Being is one of his most distinctive capacities."[50] The internal-
izing and externalizng awareness of the thirteen-year-old, for
example, begins the rich dialogue of the early adolescent with
God on something more than a purely self-centered or anthropomorphic basis. Gesell says that whereas the thirteen-year-old

"used to think of God as a person" or "half man, half spirit," he now thinks of him most often as Spirit. He will often strengthen his concept with the comment, "He's not a man."[51]

Charles Stewart studied thirty young adolescents through interviews and testing concerning their religious beliefs and practices. He tested the conclusions of Jean Piaget and Bärbel Inhelder in which they discovered that this age moves from concrete to what they call formal or logical operations in their thinking. Piaget and Inhelder said there was an increasing capacity of the young adolescent as he moves from eleven to fifteen to do abstract thinking. They formed these conclusions on the basis of the study of over fifteen hundred adolescents. In the use of a story test Stewart saw an increasing tendency toward abstract categories. From ages of twelve and a half to sixteen of his sample, over half were able to think abstractly at the age of fourteen. Yet the girls tended to think more concretely and less abstractly than did the boys.

Stewart's studies also underscore the importance of early adolescence as a time for "confronting the youth as a member of the adult religious community." In some religious communions this will be the confirmation service. The pastor, the priest, or the church school teacher becomes an identification figure for the youth and "helps bridge the gap from the primary family to the larger world through the church."[52] In churches that stress adult Baptism (although such churches tend not to have any clear-cut understanding of the relation of the preadolescent child to God and the church) early adolescence is a good time to begin the process of direct evangelism. Allport confirms this with his statement:

> Usually it is not until the stress of puberty that serious reverses occur in the evolution of the religious sentiment. At this period of development the youth is compelled to transform his religious attitudes—indeed all of his attitudes—from secondhand fittings to firsthand fittings of his personality. He can no longer let his parents do his thinking for him.[53]

In my own opinion, the whole of adolescence—from thirteen through nineteen—should be seen as an accumulative adventure in the exploration of the inner and outer world in relation to God. The early adolescent's life is characterized by longing and limitation. Upon the basis of these possibilities and necessities, he or she can, with proper leadership and open dialogue with strong adults, come to see God as creator and himself as creature, God as the ultimate fulfillment of his or her longings, and God as the one who accepts him or her as a creature with forgiveness and love.

The early adolescent's body is ripe. In it he feels the kinds of longings of which Anne Frank spoke. These longings raised to their nth degrees may be likened to the longing of Adam for a companion, the longing of the Hebrew children for deliverance, the longing of the Jews in exile for Jerusalem, and the longing of the early Christians for the return of the Lord Jesus Christ. But on a very personal level, the adolescent experiences not just longing but limitation. He wants to go, but he can only ride a bicycle. She wants to have and to hold someone close, but she will do well to have her first pair of nylon hose. They want privacy, but they are shy and confused when left alone to talk.

Anne Frank again from her diary puts it clearly as she describes the words of her boyfriend, Peter, as he began to talk to her:

> "Yes, and you see," he said, "I don't usually say anything, because I know beforehand that I'll only become tongue-tied. I begin to stutter, blush, and twist around what I want to say until I have to break off because I simply can't find the words. That's what happened yesterday, I wanted to say something quite different, but once I had started, I got in a hopeless muddle and that's frightful. I used to have a bad habit; I wish I still had it now. If I was angry with anyone rather than argue it out I would get to work on him with my fist. I quite realize that this method doesn't get me anywhere; and that is why I admire you. You are never at a loss for a word, you say exactly what you want to say to people and are never the least bit shy."

> "I can tell you, you are making a big mistake," I answered. "I usually say things quite differently from the way I meant to say them, and then I talk too much and far

too long and that's just as bad. . . . And as for me I was very pleased, because I sense a real fellowship, such as I can only remember having had with my girlfriends."[54]

Furthermore, longing and limitation in the era of adolescence focuses around money. The adolescents' pace, especially if they live in middle-class American homes, becomes more and more expensive. They long for work whereby they can earn their own money, but are limited in that few people are willing to teach them how to work, to be bothered with them, or to risk investing time and energy in training them. Then they are thrust back on the conflict between their desires and their limitations. They resort to wheedling, manipulating, driving hard bargains, etc., in order to get the money to buy the things they want. In impoverished families little wonder is it in the face of American advertisement, affluence, and adult carelessness that early adolescents begin stealing.

Longing and limitation has another quite important ethical dimension: the tendency of the early adolescent to split his or her conception of love of the opposite sex away from the experience of sex itself. Culture tends to demand this of them. Longing and limitation are thrust upon them at the same time. Harry Stack Sullivan calls this the "collisions of lust, security, and intimacy needs." The early adolescent's desire for sexual expression collides with his need for self-esteem and personal worth. The power of sexual desire and the comparative hopelessness of the early adolescent of learning how he as a particular individual can do anything about it causes the early adolescent—boy or girl—to feel inadequate, insecure, fearful. This is aided and abetted by ridicule from parents and other elders when the first signs of interest in the opposite sex appear. A more subtle form of rejection of the maturing sexual needs of the early adolescent comes in the objections, criticisms, and hindrances of the child as he moves toward members of the other sex. An even more subtle way of causing a young person to feel inadequate is to become overconcerned with and nosy about what goes on in the environs of privacy between the child and the person of the opposite sex. These really are collisions between the feeling of personal worth and the need for intimacy with a person of the opposite sex. The end-result damage is to cause the young person very early to cut the opposite sex into two groups—the sacred, maternal, loving group and the profane, sexy, worthless group. This can go either way for the boy or the girl. Even more devastating than this collision, however, is the total rejection of the whole idea of interaction between the two sexes by harsh, forbidding manners of parents, teachers, institutions, etc. In this event the groundwork is laid for early adolescents' getting into homosexual play and autosexual behavior, because the normal interaction between boys and girls is totally taboo.

SOME SUGGESTIONS
FOR PARENTS AND TEACHERS OF EARLY ADOLESCENTS

Creating Psychic Space

The early adolescent boy or girl withdraws from time to time into himself or herself. Early adolescents have brief intervals of self-absorption and rumination. It is a sort of internal psychic play. It is a constructive function. The young person may rise without a word from a family group, go to his room, and we cannot penetrate his reveries. He doesn't stay in a reverie. He moves outward toward his homework or to a project of his own. This "inwardizing" is serious business to him. Therefore, he needs "room," privacy, a thing called by some psychologists, psychic space. The early adolescent is much like a young plant that has grown as far as the container will let it grow and needs a larger pot if it is to grow farther. This gives room for the private rumination going on. This explains why the early adolescent is evasive when pressed for direct answers. If you try to interpret his feelings for him, he is likely to think that you are putting words into his mouth. As one fourteen-year-old said, "That's very unsanitary!" He is likely to think that the only person who can question him directly is his teacher who has a right to do so. When completely honest he may say that parents don't have any business knowing what he knows. The Germans have a word for this called *Lebensraum,* meaning "living space."

Parents find it hardest to do this, because they interpret the withdrawal of the child from them as rejection. They miss the closeness as parents. Likewise it is a subtle reminder that they themselves are getting older. All this makes them feel uneasy and even rejected.

The wise teacher knows that he or she is an outsider from the home to whom the young person may feel close. In realizing this the teacher can be more of an adult and less of a child. Yet even in the teacher situation we have an "occupation-centered attitude" toward youth. Each one of us wants to get our two cents' worth in. As Erik Erikson says:

> We all want to "tell them," but few of us take the time to stop and listen . . . [to what the youth] is telling us about ourselves, about youth, and about our times. . . . What the young people themselves say is often completely ignored unless they learn to say (as many do, and fast) what adults want to hear. And yet, in moments of tragic clarity, they themselves express most succinctly what otherwise only our complex theories of unconscious motivation can even begin to grasp.[55]

Manners and Morals

I asked my own fourteen-year-old son what he felt a fourteen-year-old boy or girl most needed to know. His first reaction, after having asked for the day in which to think about it, was that they most needed to know what the right kind of manners are, especially in social groups where there are both boys and girls. This gives me a whole new perception of what kind of boy-girl instruction is most needed. They worry about how to start a conversation with each other, how to be sure to do the kinds of things that please each other, and how to plan such things as a birthday party, a response to a young girl's invitation to a party at her house, etc. Parents and teachers can offset the collision between the need for intimacy and the need for participation with the opposite sex in several ways by taking this appeal for the right way to do things seriously. Both parent and teacher can certainly refrain from ridicule and crude humor, getting in the way of detectable movements of the child toward members of the other sex, and invading the private fantasies of their thoughts and feelings about the opposite sex.

Sublimation has become so commonly used that its real meaning has been lost. It does not mean breaking up efforts at communication between the sexes, and diverting this concern to such things as poetry, art, "cloud" music, and sentimental overglorifications of sex. Rather, sublimation means creating opportunities whereby people of the opposite sex may have legitimate, socially acceptable, and happily responsible fellowship with each other. This is usually done with earlier adolescents by creating group opportunities where both boys and girls can have fellowship with each other. These opportunities most certainly should be in a context of play and work where they can even have some bodily contact with each other. An excellent example is a swimming party. The local "sock hop" at the high school is another example. Body contact sports such as touch football are often played by both boys and girls although I am sure there is enough fear among the average church congregation to cause much of this behavior to go unappreciated. Nevertheless, the young person keenly wants an opportunity to learn how to relate himself and herself effectively and appropriately in good manners toward the opposite sex.

Early adolescence is a ripe time for the teaching of the physiology of the human organism in the context of the Biblical doctrine of the wholeness of personality. Flesh and spirit should be taught as different dimensions of the one person. They are not unconsecrated enemies of each other. Such teaching provides another opportunity for the elision rather than the collision of the concept of sex with the worship of God. The Committee on Weekday Christian Education Curriculum of the National Council of Churches rightly emphasizes that human life and experience resist compartmentalization and can be truly seen and evaluated only in a framework of total and ultimate meaning. Persons are whole and cannot be logically or psychologically divided. Love—whether it be sexual love, parental love, or the love of God—involves sacrifice and suffering, responsibility and trust. For early adolescents the pamphlet by Marion O. Lerrigo and Helen Southard, entitled *Finding Yourself,* is published by the American Medical Association, 535 North Dearborn Street, Chicago, Ill.

60610. Another fine volume is Eric W. Johnson's book *Love and Sex in Plain Language,* published by J. B. Lippincott Company in 1965.

The Wonderful World of Color

One of the happiest phenomena of television and motion pictures is the work of Walt Disney. To young and old alike he introduces the variegated color and action of the world. This may be taken as a parable of the need of early adolescents in their moral reeducation. By the time a young person has reached thirteen to sixteen years of age he has learned many of the values of our culture. Ordinarily they have been taught to him in such a way that the world is colorless—everything is "black, black bad" or "white, white good." As O. S. English and G. H. J. Pearson say:

> The average American adolescent is unprepared for the imperfections of the real world and so is disillusioned when he meets it. The inconsistencies, even of the people who taught the ideals, are picked out unmercifully by the adolescent. Furthermore, American adolescents do not have a uniform basis of mores, taboos, and customs for reference. . . . There is no single set of ideals on which the adolescent can depend.[56]

Therefore, both the parent and the teacher can raise the early adolescent's level of vulnerability and stress, increase his capacity to tolerate frustration, and sharpen his awareness of individual and group differences between various kinds of people if they are flexible enough to do so. As one early adolescent said: "We should be schooled in religion in an open and free way, so that we can talk back. We should not be told: 'Now look, you fellows, Jesus did this and Jesus did that, and so that's that. Keep your big mouth shut.'" The need for dialogue begins to appear in early adolescence. If parents and teachers do not "tap in" on this need early, the only source of consistency and solidarity the early adolescent can find is from his fellow gang members. Group formation really becomes possible in early adolescence. If there are weak identifications or no identification at all with adults, the group becomes the early adolescent's only point of reference in a very confusing and conflicting world of values. Misconduct is likely to be the price of belonging to his own age group. "The purpose of the gang or group is to repudiate adult influence and strengthen the individual's inner feelings of capability by his close association with his peers."[57]

The teacher or parent who knows and acts upon his knowledge can turn the moral confusion around young people into fruitful growth for the early adolescent by establishing a steady initiative of concern for them as individuals. An adolescent told me that his teacher "just sees the class as a group" and never as individuals. The only way, he says, a person can become an individual to the teacher is "sitting on the front row, waving one's hand and asking stupid questions, hanging around after class, starting a ruckus in the class, or to be always apple-polishing the teacher."

The very character of the gospel is built upon aggressive initiative. God took the initiative toward us in Christ. As a corporate body of mankind he came to us as individuals. In Christ he wills that we become children of God, each with a varied uniqueness of his own. In such a Christian context there will be a pluralism of religious forms, cultural values, and standards of behavior. These variations never come in cleft colors of black and white. They come in the many-colored hues of the wonderful world of color known as humankind. The Lord Jesus Christ empties himself of himself and takes upon himself the form of any of us who believe on him. Among Christians there are varieties of gifts. Even though all things are not expedient, all things are lawful. The opening of the Spirit between teacher and pupil and between pupil and pupil creates an atmosphere in which the many varieties of behavior and Christian values can be inspected, assessed, appreciated, and criticized.

Yet a common bond holds the children of God together: We are created in the image of God; we are persons for whom Christ died; we must decide for ourselves what is right under God.

Chapter X

LATE ADOLESCENCE: AN AGE OF DREAMING, SEEKING, STRIVING, TAMING

I DID NOT KNOW until I consulted an unabridged dictionary that there is a verb "adolesce," meaning "to grow up." We have a way of speaking to persons of *all* age groups: "Why don't you grow up?" Many answers can, upon reflection, be given to this question. First, people don't grow *up*, because people around them hold them *down*. They treat them as children. Second, they do not grow up because they are afraid of failing at adult responsibilities. Third, they do not grow up because their particular *rate* of growing is not exactly the rate of others around them. They have their own pace. Fourth, they do not grow up because they think it is more comfortable not to make decisions and change. Fifth, they do not grow up because in *not* doing this they create anger in people who in their frustration ask hostilely: "Why don't you grow up?"

ADOLESCING: A PATTERN OF ACTION

Early adolescence ushers a young person into a new *status* in life. He or she is a teen-ager now. Much of the earlier years of adolescence is spent in reveling over having *become* something new. We long and strain against limits. We do not have adequate religious ceremonies with which to celebrate and interpret this new status in life. Yet we have a barrage of radio, television, movies, newspaper, and popular magazine interpretations of this event. This moves from Pat Boone, the Beatles, the Monkees, etc., to such items as "I Was a Teen-age Werewolf"! One hesitates to write these titles down. By the time this reaches print, the reader will have a whole new set of names instead.

Yet, do not hear me as despising utterly all these antics of our culture to describe the action-centered population known as teen-agers. I am not. In church, the adolescent *sits, listens,* and the nearest thing to *appropriate* action he can get is *looking.* He does much of this. But in the ever-changing dance forms, identification with athletic and entertainment idols, the young person *moves.* Growing up is an active verb. He is "intoxicated" with locomotion. Thus acting out rather than speaking up characterizes late adolescence. The young person adolesces all over the place! To his teachers and parents, adolescence is a state of being. To the young person it is a process of becoming. What are some of the things the late adolescent *does* to signal his growing up, his becoming? How are these *acts* related to his or her becoming a child of God?

DREAMING

Erikson rightly says that "among the necessary ingredients of adolescing is experimentation with the borderline between fantasy and reality."[58] The healthy adolescent has an active dreaming capacity, i.e., whether awake or asleep he can go far and deep into an elaborate fantasy world. I can recall as a teen-ager myself being fascinated by the mystery of a movie called *Just Imagine.* The unheard-of inventions of the future —most of which are commonplace to my teen-age sons now— were to me a dreamy, unimaginable sort of thing.

The Biblical personality of the dreamer is Joseph. At seventeen, his brothers had to sit still out of fear of their father, but Joseph told them his fantastic dreams. They were to "bow down" to him. Even the sun, the moon, and eleven stars were to bow down to him. "They said one to another, 'Here comes this dreamer.' " (Gen. 37:19.)

Joseph was given a "long robe with sleeves" by his father as a symbol of the father's preference for him. Joseph catered to authority. He brought evil reports of his brothers to his father. He thereby broke his relationship with his own age group in behalf of the approval of the "older generation." He became a dreamer, but his brothers represented reality to him. A contemporary psychotherapist has designated this "dreamer" quality of late adolescence as "omnipotentiality." He defines this word:

> It consists primarily of the feeling and conviction on the part of the youth that he can do anything in the world, solve any problem in the world if given the opportunity. And if it is not given, he will create it. . . . He can indulge in wild flights of imagination, soaring speculations, incredible adventures. He knows no limits in fantasy, and accepts grudgingly any limits in reality. Yet he finds it difficult to do one thing and follow it through to completion, because to do so would mean to commit himself to one thing primarily, and this he is not yet prepared to do.[59]

This dilemma of youth between dreams and unpreparedness for commitment to one thing is especially true of middle-class families. They push their children hard to "make up their mind," "to choose a vocation," to take just the right subjects in school "that they are going to need later on in college or graduate school," etc.

DREAM-FOCUSING

Yet while all this preoccupation with reality is going on in the adult, parent, and even older siblings, the sixteen- to nineteen-year-old is preoccupied with his dreams. They are punctuated with power symbols. The most important focus of these dreams is the national ritual of "getting a driver's license" and driving a car. At this point dream and reality collide with each other. In middle and upper classes, the whole relationship of the father to the young person changes when the youth gets a driver's license. Earlier, the relationship to the mother changed radically when the infant became a child by learning to walk. Now, the father—whose own ego is involved in the family car too—finds that *he* is involved and cannot just avoid the demands of his child by saying, "Go ask your mother." He is in it "for real" now. Within the home the car is the point of contact between the dreams of power, speed, and liberty in the youth and the reality-fears of the law, of accidents, of expense, and even death in the parent. In poverty-stricken families, the temptation to steal or "borrow" a car for its own sake is great.

The church makes too little or nothing at all of the religious and ethical significance of driving a car. Yet, getting a driver's license may mean more to the late adolescent than his Baptism, confirmation, or his graduation from high school. The removal of the privilege of "being on wheels" when he goes to college is a bigger readjustment than not having home cooking. The high school ritualizes this in driver training courses. This creative point of contact between the adult and adolescent is loaded with possibilities for collaboration or conflict between the two. For the need of the late adolescent is not more rules and frustration from adults. His need is for one-to-one collaboration—not dictation or domination—with a trusted adult. That adult cannot just relive his own adolescence. He cannot writhe in jealousy of the youth and the energy of the adolescent. He cannot force too early a commitment. An elaborate array of "possibilities" must be "tried on" for size. This feeling of dreaming, "omnipotentiality," must be permitted as the teen-ager roams "far and wide in many fields before responding to the social and maturational necessity of commitment." The adult can collaborate in this process.

As a professor who teaches theological students, I see the results when the church and family of my students have "programmed" them into premature commitments to the Christian ministry. This makes them, for a time, the favorite son of their parents and church. However, they are either spoiled rotten with favoritism or so overcommitted to the role of being a minister that they have trouble learning how to *function* as a minister. Yet their fellow students, assigned the task of leading the sheep, too, as were Joseph's brothers, tend to be the whetstone of reality against which the student is sharpened by a wise professor. Much has been said about why ministers leave the ministry. One reason is that they were pushed into premature commitments. They later regress to late adolescence—uncommitment. The other options of life must be real to them before they can honestly *become* ministers.

How the Church
Can Guide the Adolescing Process

The church can do two important things to aid in the collaborative process with late adolescents.

The Ritual of Age Sixteen

First, the churches can provide a ritual and an interpretation of the sixteenth birth date of their youth. This can be focused around their getting their driver's licenses. Law enforcement officers could be involved in the ceremony. Parents and younger children should be present. Commitment of one area of life is the resolute decision to look with reverence upon the "right" to drive a car. The age ranges for the privilege of driving a car differ from state to state in this country. This in itself is confusing to youths. Driving should be interpreted not as an automatic "right" at a given age, but a privilege calling for education, discipline, and a sense of responsibility not only to others but before God. Youth camps, retreats, vacation church schools, etc., could involve the youths in the study of an automobile. As an early adolescent needs to know how his or her body works, even so does the late adolescent need to know how an automobile works. As the radio and television with which a young person became accustomed earlier are extensions of his senses, especially his eyes and ears, the automobile is an extension of his muscles, feet, legs, and human power. When we realize that more Americans are killed by automobiles than in war, one wonders why it is that the moral fervor of the church can be mobilized about the wrongness of war, and yet the church cannot develop concern about a prior discipline. For example, high school education in driver skill and responsibility are not espoused as *moral* causes by the churches. Much subtle and even unconscious motivation surrounds this event. The church through ritual and moral instruction should bring moral causes to light. "In addition to being a symbol of masculine success, the automobile or its function [is] a symbol of, or a substitute for, feminine goals," says one psychotherapist. The car activates the interest of the girlfriend *and* the mother of a boy. It appeals to the male need to compete with other males. It focuses conflict with fathers. It should be an avenue of access to the church's communication with the late adolescent. Becoming a child of God today is a process which—whether we like it or not—is partially symbolized in the automobile today —not sheep, camels, or horses.[60]

The Ritual of the First Job

A second ritual follows "getting wheels" as day follows the night: "getting money." The late adolescent is made to feel like a child when asking parents for money for gasoline, for dates, for food bought in restaurants and not eaten at home. He or she can "try on" many "possibilities" for life by doing different kinds of work for money. This can begin ever so gently in the home by the parents asking the teen-ager to watch the plumber fix the leaky faucets and learn how to do it. The next time the faucets leak he can fix them. A daughter can learn to sew and make money by pocketing a portion of what she saves.

The "job bit" can grow somewhat more completely as the neighborhood provides grass-cutting, tree-trimming, roof-fixing, window-washing, baby-sitting, etc., jobs. Neighbors often run businesses and can begin the process of teaching the youth a trade. The trade should normally *precede* the vocation. Working with their hands is an excitement to many youths. Construction work seems to have a particular mystique for some boys. Creative hobbies such as music, art, photography, boating, swimming, tennis, and golf often "flower out" into money-making opportunities. A combo band, arts and crafts work in a camp or a hospital, work in a camera shop, a swim club, or a country club, etc., becomes a "live option" for a place to work.

The teacher who is "tuned in" to the signals of young people will be sensitive to their appeals for work. Usually these are short-term, part-time, or occasional commitments. They do not call for "big" decisions. They do provide experiences into which a young person may peer to find himself. They provide money and a measure of dignity in independence. Commitment to these may be brief but deep.

The official board of a church is often made up of employers of one kind or another. A church should be like the United States Navy personnel and have as their ingroup motto: "The Navy looks after its own." The church should have this motto of looking after its own young people's needs for jobs. I can bear witness personally to the great benefit and pleasure that came to my late-teen-age son when one of the lay leaders approached him and simply told him quietly that he "had a job for him." A pastor and three of his lay leaders in another church organized the high school and college students eligible for work during the summer. They successfully placed all of them. They had a breakfast meeting with them once a week for prayer, group interchange, and inspiration before they went on their jobs that day. Youths unrelated to the church can be met in or out of the church on a common ground of a known need for work. They are more likely to see what the church is all about if the lay community takes interest in their concerns for work. Naturally some youths do not need the assistance of the church in this particular way of employment counseling. They prefer to "go it on their own." But even these persons enjoy being congratulated and noticed when they have "done something on their own." The inquiring and caring church becomes aware of their independence of spirit and provides attentive encouragement for their efforts.

The church that is in the inner city can move even more carefully and seriously in the employment counseling of youths. The high school dropout is usually looking for a job and thinks he can do much more "on his own" than he really can. The young delinquent returned to the community has trouble finding a job because of his record. The church that takes seriously the attitude of youths toward cars, money, and work will find that attitude is no respecter of the particular part of the city it is in. It simply takes different forms.

The rituals of job-finding are mysteries to the average late adolescent, but he grows almost visibly as he learns these from adults. The ministry of intercession with other adults for the late adolescent is one never forgotten by a grateful youth. We as adults have so focused on recreation for youth that we have missed their need for work. Public recreation facilities can outdo us here. But the autonomy that comes with having their own money is a gift of dignity a church can bring into being for youth. This brings their dreams into touch with reality.

SEEKING

Dreaming is one part of adolescing. Seeking is another. As has been said, the late adolescent is not ready to "set in concrete" once and for all his life commitments. As he "casts about" restlessly through infancy, childhood, and early adolescence, he comes to feel most at ease when he knows clearly what he means to others. He or she has an identity, a place, an estimate for himself or herself. Yet this comes as a gift (or curse) from others and is not distinctly his own or her own choice. Finding out for oneself who one is by choice is the search upon which the adolescent is thrust. This takes some time, a "parenthesis" in human achievement. How shall we describe this time of quest, this opportunity to search?

A Time of Fallowing

Spafford Ackerly, professor emeritus of psychiatry at the University of Louisville School of Medicine, calls late adolescence "a lying fallow period of consolidation." This is a figure of speech from farming. A piece of land is plowed up in order to destroy the weeds. Then it is allowed to rest and no crop is planted. Thus, it renews itself by fallowing. The ground, though not producing a crop, undergoes an active bacteriological and chemical process leading to regeneration. Professor Ackerly indicts our generation for devaluing the importance of idealism and hero worship. By doing this, "we have left our adolescents confused between the executors of conformity and the exploiters of non-conformity, with no one to support their extravagant, unbridled and precious reaching after the stars."[61] The fallowing period is one in which the adolescing youth is not to be hurried. It "precedes the assumption of the responsibilities of occupation, love, marriage, and children. Something is needed before playing for keeps. . . . It is another period of play, only this time with intellectual concepts, holding off closure or solidification in any particular direction."[62] Ackerly

cites Lincoln running a grocery store with few customers, rumi-
nating in uninterrupted thought. George Bernard Shaw spent
ages twenty to twenty-eight "in solitude away from family,
friends, and business career," to quote Shaw himself. This
"lying fallow is not a 'do nothing' state, but an uneasy serenity
holding off the comfort of ritualization, of premature closure
of judgment."[63]

This is equally true of heavy closure of religious commitments. My own feeling is that a steady accumulation of specific
rituals of "becoming" is better than the overloading of *one*
decision to be a Christian. I feel that an openness should be
maintained by adults about religious convictions so that even
the most precious of these beliefs can be a discussible or even
debatable topic of concern. The "no" precedes the "yes" with
many late adolescents. Unless the "no" is heard, the "yes" may
be held with inner reservations.

Therefore, having a teacher, a parent, an adult friend who
understands—whom the late adolescent can trust—may make
all the difference. James Agee had such a teacher in Father
Flye, with whom he corresponded. Agee wrote Father Flye
about his own work as a poet:

> One thing I feel is this: that a great deal of poetry is the
> product of adolescence—or of an emotionally adolescent
> frame of mind: and that as this state of mind changes,
> poetry is likely to dry up. I think most people let it.[64]

Ackerly insists that this "state of mind" should—to some
extent—characterize us throughout life. This is what a real
vacation is. As more and more people enter retirement, this
frame of mind is a gift that supports us "against the vacuous-
ness of old age." The child of God must have a "place" deep
inside himself where he can rest "from the burning of the
noontide heat, and the burden of the day." That place is made
during the "fallowing" of life.

A Psychosocial Moratorium

Erik Erikson characterizes the era of later adolescence as a
"moratorium," a delay granted to somebody not ready to meet
an obligation. He asks for a "selective permissiveness on the

part of society and provocative playfulness on the part of youth."[65] The individual's identity formation calls for time out from the accustomed demands of his family, culture, church, and school. The lower-lower-class youth may take time out from the chaos, shifting, and drifting of his family. The middle-class youth may take time out from making "A's," going to Sunday school, and planning for college. The upper-class youth may take time out from affluence, social ritual, and the family business.

Military service often provides late adolescent boys the cultural rationale for getting their moratorium. College students quite often deliberately enter military service "in order to find themselves." During the Middle Ages young persons went on Crusades. Today they may enter the Peace Corps, join a "rights" movement, or simply goof off, to the despair of un-understanding parents and status-conscious friends of the family. Many consciously relish the suspension of decision and concomitant adventure of military service.

Tragedies of Late Adolescence

Yet we live in a time when young persons are "programmed" from their first squawk as babies newborn until they hear the first squawk of their own children. Then they are often left with no guidance. They are pushed into earlier and earlier adult commitments. In my own denomination—one that supposedly insists on adult conversions—the age level of such religious decisions is younger. The entrance of the sputnik age has sought to make young scientists overnight. The *avant-garde* approaches to advanced programs in high schools and colleges seek to make intellectuals out of late and delayed adolescents. They often become "cakes not turned," to use Hosea's figure of speech for Ephraim (Hos. 7:8).

When this happens, the moratorium, the fallowing period, comes by force and not by permission. The organisms of young people convulse. They become sick or delinquent. Their own uniqueness is cooked wrongly in the hustling heat of production, achievement, and success. Then hospitalization and correctional schools become a moratorium of another kind. The damage may or may not be undone. As Erik Erikson says of George Bernard Shaw, "He broke loose to avoid the danger of success without identity." So late adolescents today are "breaking loose." Often their illnesses are transitional personality disorders aimed to accomplish unconsciously in isolation what family and community will not permit them to accomplish consciously and in fellowship with understanding adults.

The Quest for Identity

Another way of characterizing the seeking quality of late adolescents is what Alan Wheelis calls "the quest for identity." An earlier generation afforded final and complete, rigid and fixed, rules for the succeeding generation. Identity was *fixed* to occupations. However, today occupations shift. Personal identity remains fluid and changing. "Commitments of all kinds—social, vocational, marital—are made more tentatively. Long-term goals seem to become progressively less feasible."[66]

Therefore, the young person today faces the temporariness of that which his elders, especially his grandparents, looked upon as unchangeable entities: vocational roles, marital bonds, ethical standards, and religious beliefs. He is called upon to exercise faith in the face of the unknown rather than to accept fixed ideas, permanent job assignments, unthreatened marriage contract, and universally agreed upon religious doctrines. He has to go on a pilgrimage, a quest, a search for *his* identity. Then it does not come to him in the form of a rose-trellised cottage, with wife and child waiting in certainty of schedule as he returns from the kind of work his father and grandfather did before him. No. His identity comes to him as a cloud by day and a pillar of fire by night. He goes out, not knowing where he goes, not knowing when or whither he will get back. This is the nature of his time of fallowing, his psychosocial moratorium, his quest for identity. Yet—he is called. The call cannot be denied. It, too, has a *must* about it that saves it from the "mustiness" of a fixed "thing to do." It has all the playful seriousness about it of which John Masefield speaks in more than one of his poems, but especially clear is it in his "Sea Fever." He speaks of the call of the sea to a person's destiny as follows:

I must down to the seas again, for the call of the running tide
Is a wild call and a clear call that may not be denied.[67]

STRIVING

The seeking of late adolescing has an internal witness of the Holy Spirit in it. The youth must *on his own* kindle the gift of God that is within him. He must have the playful freedom to do so. Yet the patterning of life falls into place as he or she is permitted to strive as well as to dream and to seek. The privilege of making their own mistakes is an inalienable right of all young people. The water beyond the edge of the beach is deep. If they are to stay afloat, they must kick their own legs and make their own arm strokes. Granted this effort, the water is their friend. Denied this right and responsibility, they are engulfed. But no one can *swim for* them.

Gordon Allport, professor of psychology at Harvard, says that personality regularly has a characteristic feature of *striving*. Far from reducing tension and anxiety, striving maintains it and generates it. Striving makes for the unification of personality. Striving has a future reference. Life is *understood* by evaluating one's history and present situation. Life is *lived* in terms of one's interests, expectations, planning, and intentions.[68]

From this vantage point, commitment is weighed in terms of the short-term and long-range intentions of life. In the welter of many dry runs, false starts, and experimentations with life, the emerging young adult—given patience, information, understanding, and steadfast ties of affection from teacher, parent, and pastor—tends to find himself. *His* or *her* way of striving may seem "crazy"; but so did Edison's. The commitment may be short-lived, but it was deep while it lasted. So was John F. Kennedy's. But Allport insists that these seemingly crazy and short-lived enthusiasms of youth may well be at the center of their long-range intentions in life. He cites Roald Amundsen who from the age of fifteen had one dominant passion, to be a polar explorer. He was tempted to forget it, reduce the tension of the passion, and live "like other people live." He resisted the temptation. He kept this commitment and died rescuing a less gifted explorer.[69]

The task of the teacher is to perceive these "stubborn strivings" of the young person with a mind of his own. This raises the question, as Kenneth Harris does, of how serious we are about our task as teachers:

> If we believe in the future, we must believe in the capacity of our children to create that future. I do not view today's youngsters with alarm. It is said they are blasé. I do not think so. I think they despise false sentiment; I think they can spot a phony better than we could. I think if you want to move them emotionally—if you want to make their hearts throb—you had better have a throbbing heart when you get up to talk to them.
>
> If young people seem blasé and indifferent, I think it is because we have not touched their hearts with worthy motives in which we ourselves deeply believe.
>
> Somewhere in your schools are tomorrow's potential Robert Frost, Marie Curie, Thomas Wolfe, Andrew Wyeth. They don't know it, and they may never know it unless you are able to hold before them a clear image of what constitutes true greatness—true success.
>
> I envy you that task, because no one else has, at the same time, so great an opportunity.[70]

Spafford Ackerly dramatizes our task even further in the conclusion of his article:

> Antoine de Saint-Exupéry, in *Wind, Sand and Stars*—you will remember the airplane pilot's early morning bus ride to the airport and his description of the humble meditations of worn-out clerks who talked only of illness, money and shabby domestic cares, and his reaction in these words: "Old Bureaucrat, my Comrade, it is not you who are to blame, no one ever helped you to escape. You, like a termite, built your peace by blocking up with cement your every chink and cranny through which the light might pierce. You rolled yourself up into a ball in your genteel security; in routine; in the stifling conventions of provincial life. Raising a rampart against the winds and the tides and the stars. You have chosen not to be perturbed by great problems. You are not the dweller upon an errant planet and do not ask yourself questions to which there are no answers. Nobody grasped you by the shoulder while there was still time. Now naught in you

will ever awaken the sleeping musician, the poet, the
astronomer that possibly inhabited you in the beginning.
The squall has ceased to be a cause of my complaint. The
magic of this craft of the air has opened for me a world
in which I shall confront, within two hours, the black
dragons and the crowned crests of a comet of blue light-
nings, and when night has fallen, I, delivered from the
storm, shall read my course in the stars."

Is not the author saying, hold off and do not solidify your ideas
and behavior into final patterns too early by being afraid of
change and the complexity of things; cultivate flexibility and
loving concern for one's fellowman; welcome the beauty of
the storm and the challenge of great truths?—a poet's hints on
how man might better fulfill himself.[71]

TAMING

The dreaming, the seeking, and the striving of the late adolescent makes a sort of "wild thing" of him or her. "There's no
telling what they will do next," we say.

This "wildness" is both exciting and frightening. The lack
of center, direction, and stability is challenged by three "civilizing" forces of life: (1) the need of a child born to the emerging young adult for a secure and steadfast pair of parents; (2)
the encouragement and enrichment of the lives of parents by
the church and community in order that they may more nearly
approximate being "steadfast and secure parents"; and (3) the
need of the emerging young adult both to become a leader himself and to be led by others.

The taming or civilizing process, then, is a *three*-front crisis
of identity—sexual identity, basic-belief identity, and leadership identity. These commitments, being human, are frail,
fragile, and temporary as life itself. Yet they are the core of a
person's identity. They call for "ties that bind." The original
meaning of religion is "to bind." Religious faith is a commitment of the total self to Christ. We are bound by our commitment. We are in bondage to Christ. We choose him as our
Leader. The Leader and the led are bound to each other. Man
and woman are bound to each other in the oneness of sexual

union. These are ties. They bind. The teacher-pupil relationship binds them to each other. We participate with late adolescents as they settle upon the beliefs, mates, and ideas that are
to be theirs.

Antoine de Saint-Exupéry tells the delightful story of the
little prince and the fox. The fox was looking for someone "to
tame" him. The little prince was looking for a friend:

Said the little prince, "I am looking for friends. What
does that mean—'tame'?"

"It is an act too often neglected," said the fox. "It
means to establish ties."

" 'To establish ties'?"

"Just that," said the fox. "To me, you are still nothing
more than a little boy who is just like a hundred thousand other little boys. And I have no need of you. And
you, on your part, have no need of me. To you, I am
nothing more than a fox like a hundred thousand other
foxes. But if you tame me, then we shall need each other.
To me, you will be unique in all the world. To you, I
shall be unique in all the world . . ."

"My life is very monotonous," he said. "I hunt chickens; men hunt me. All the chickens are just alike, and all
the men are just alike. And, in consequence, I am a little
bored. But if you tame me, it will be as if the sun came to
shine on my life. I shall know the sound of a step that will
be different from all the others. Other steps send me hur-
rying back underneath the ground. Yours will call me,
like music, out of my burrow. And then look: you see the
grain-fields down yonder? I do not eat bread. Wheat is
of no use to me. The wheat fields have nothing to say to
me. And that is sad. But you have hair that is the color
of gold. Think how wonderful that will be when you have
tamed me! The grain, which is also golden, will bring me
back the thought of you. And I shall love to listen to the
wind in the wheat . . ."

The fox gazed at the little prince, for a long time.

"Please—tame me!" he said.

"I want to, very much," the little prince replied. "But
I have not much time. I have friends to discover, and a
great many things to understand."

"One only understands the things that one tames," said the fox. "Men have no more time to understand anything. They buy things all ready made at the shops. But there is no shop anywhere where one can buy friendship, and so men have no friends any more. If you want a friend, tame me . . ."

"What must I do, to tame you?" asked the little prince.

"You must be very patient," replied the fox. "First you will sit down at a little distance from me—like that—in the grass. I shall look at you out of the corner of my eye, and you will say nothing. Words are the source of mis-understandings. But you will sit a little closer to me, every day . . ."

The next day the little prince came back.

"It would have been better to come back at the same hour," said the fox. "If, for example, you come at four o'clock in the afternoon, then at three o'clock I shall be-gin to be happy. I shall feel happier and happier as the hour advances. At four o'clock, I shall already be worry-ing and jumping about. I shall show you how happy I am! But if you come at just any time, I shall never know at what hour my heart is to be ready to greet you . . . One must observe the proper rites . . ."

"What is a rite?" asked the little prince.

"Those also are actions too often neglected," said the fox. "They are what make one day different from other days, one hour from other hours. There is a rite, for ex-ample, among my hunters. Every Thursday they dance with the village girls. So Thursday is a wonderful day for me! I can take a walk as far as the vineyards. But if the hunters danced at just any time, every day would be like every other day, and I should never have any vacation at all."[72]

Fidelity: The Central Virtue of Adolescence

"Coming every Thursday at the same time"—that is fidelity. Fidelity is the main virtue of both early and late adolescents. This is the hallmark of the genuine Christian, the child of God —he is faithful. We are not called to be successes, millionaires, or geniuses. These may come. But we *are* called to be "good and faithful servants of Jesus Christ." The childlike element of trust is reactivated in the late adolescent in the form of fidelity to long-range relationships to people, beliefs, and purposes. The central quality of becoming children of God rests here. We live in a restless and changing world but our faith in God may, as Allport says, confer marked integration upon personality. "A man's religion is his audacious bid . . . to bind himself to creation and The Creator."[73]

In our fearful wildness, we are like untamed foxes. We deeply want to be tamed. From another realm has come a Prince who was little but grew as we grow. He is not too busy to understand. He established ties with us by taking time to become as we are. He became as we are that through faith in him we might become as he is. To us as Christians he is unique in all the world for this reason. To him, we shall be unique in all the world. "To all who receive him, who believe in his name, he gives power to become children of God." (See John 1:12.) "What love the Father has given us, that we should be called children of God; and so we are." (I John 3:1.)

NOTES

1. Walt Whitman, "There Was a Child Went Forth," *Leaves of Grass* (Modern Library Edition), p. 228.

2. Margaret A. Ribble, *The Rights of Infants: Early Psychological Needs and Their Satisfaction*, 2d ed. (Columbia University Press, 1965), pp. 10–12.

3. Erik H. Erikson, *Identity and the Life Cycle* (International Universities Press, Inc., 1959), p. 64.

4. *Ibid.*, p. 65.

5. Lewis J. Sherrill, *The Struggle of the Soul* (The Macmillan Company, 1951), pp. 23–24.

6. Robert J. Havighurst, *Developmental Tasks and Education*, 2d ed. (David McKay Company, 1952), p. 5.

7. George Arthur Buttrick and others (eds.), *The Interpreter's Bible* (Abingdon Press, 1952), Vol. VIII, p. 471.

8. Ribble, *op. cit.*, pp. 10–12.

9. Howard Rome, "Love Is a Very Light Thing," from the Broadway musical *Fanny*.

10. R. A. Spitz, *No and Yes: On the Genesis of Human Communication* (International Universities Press, Inc., 1957). Quoted by Gordon W. Allport, *Pattern and Growth in Personality* (Holt, Rinehart and Winston, Inc., 1961), p. 112.

11. Gordon W. Allport, *Pattern and Growth in Personality* (Holt, Rinehart and Winston, Inc., 1961), p. 114.

12. Erikson, *Identity and the Life Cycle*, p. 89.

13. Allport, *Pattern and Growth in Personality*, p. 115.

14. Martin Buber, *Images of Good and Evil* (London: Routledge & Kegan Paul, Ltd., 1952), pp. 82–83.

15. Paul Tillich, *On the Boundary* (Charles Scribner's Sons, 1966), p. 14.

16. Paul Johnson, *Person and Counselor* (Abingdon Press, 1967), p. 154.

17. Edward Sapir, *Language: An Introduction to the Study of Speech* (Harcourt, Brace & Co., Inc., 1949), p. 4.

18. Jean Piaget, *The Language and Thought of the Child* (Meridian Books, 1955), pp. 32 ff.

19. Lewis J. Sherrill and Helen H. Sherrill, *Becoming a Christian: A Manual for Communicant Classes* (John Knox Press, 1943), pp. 141–142.

20. Diane Long, David Elkind, and Bernard Spilka, "The Child's Conception of Prayer," *The Journal of the Scientific Study of Religion*, Vol. VI, No. 1 (Spring, 1967), pp. 101–109.

21. See the footnote on p. 121 of Gordon Allport, *Pattern and Growth in Personality*.

22. William Healy, A. F. Bronner, and A. M. Bowers, *The Structure and Meaning of Psychoanalysis* (Alfred A. Knopf, Inc., 1930), pp. 330–332.

23. Jean Piaget, *The Construction of Reality in the Child* (Basic Books, Inc., Publishers, 1954), pp. 354–355.

24. Alfred North Whitehead, *Religion in the Making* (The Macmillan Company, 1926), p. 16.

25. Nicolas Berdyaev, *Dream and Reality* (Collier Books, 1950), p. 44.

26. *Ibid.*, pp. 45–47.

27. George Arthur Buttrick and others (eds.), *The Interpreter's Bible*, Vol. II, p. 684a.

28. Erik H. Erikson, *Childhood and Society*, rev. ed. (W. W. Norton & Company, Inc., 1963), p. 255.

29. Erikson, *Identity and the Life Cycle*, p. 80.

30. Oscar Hammerstein, *The King and I* (Random House, Inc., 1951).

31. Oscar Hammerstein and Joshua Logan, *South Pacific: A Musical Play* (Random House, Inc., 1949).

32. Erikson, *Identity and the Life Cycle*, p. 82.

33. Harry Stack Sullivan, *The Interpersonal Theory of Psychiatry*, ed. by Helen Swick Perry and Mary Ladd Gawel (W. W. Norton & Company, Inc., 1953), p. 229.

34. *Ibid.*, p. 237.

35. *Ibid.*, p. 242.

36. Erikson, *Identity and the Life Cycle*, p. 87.

37. Elizabeth Nowell (ed.), *The Letters of Thomas Wolfe* (Charles Scribner's Sons, 1956), pp. 122–123.

38. Gaines S. Dobbins, *Great Teachers Make a Difference* (Broadman Press, 1965), p. 90.

39. Sullivan, *The Interpersonal Theory of Psychiatry*, p. 245.

40. Harry Stack Sullivan, *Conceptions of Modern Psychiatry* (Washington: William Alanson White Psychiatric Foundation, 1947), p. 55.

41. *Ibid.*, p. 248.

42. Mary Chase, *Mrs. McThing* (Oxford University Press, Inc., 1952), p. 105.

43. Robert A. Blebs *et al.*, *Counseling with Teenagers* (Prentice-Hall, Inc., 1965), p. 21.

44. Arnold Gesell, Francis Ilg, and Louise Ames, *Youth: The Years from Ten to Sixteen* (Harper & Row, Publishers, Inc., 1956), pp. 148–149.

45. Sigmund Freud, *Collected Papers*, 2d ed. (London: Hogarth Press, Ltd., 1943), Vol. III, p. 597.

46. Charles Stewart, *Adolescent Religion: A Developmental Study of the Religion of Youth* (Abingdon Press, 1967), p. 296.

47. Gesell, Ilg, and Ames, *op. cit.*, pp. 148–149.

48. Anne Frank, *The Diary of a Young Girl* (Doubleday & Company, Inc., Pocket Cardinal Edition, 1952), p. 120.

49. Gordon Allport, *Becoming: Basic Considerations for a Psychology of Personality* (Yale University Press, 1955), p. 94.

50. *Ibid.*, p. 98.

51. Gesell, Ilg, and Ames, *op. cit.*, p. 173.

52. Stewart, *op. cit.*, pp. 175–176, 184.

53. Gordon Allport, *The Individual and His Religion* (The Macmillan Company, 1950), p. 32.

54. Frank, *op. cit.*, pp. 135–136.

55. H. L. Witmer and R. Kotinsky (eds.), *New Perspectives for Research on Juvenile Delinquency* (U.S. Government Printing Office, 1955), p. 3.

56. O. S. English and G. H. J. Pearson, *Emotional Problems of Living: Avoiding the Neurotic Pattern*, 3d ed. (W. W. Norton & Company, Inc., 1963), pp. 362–363.

57. *Ibid.*

58. Witmer and Kotinsky (eds.), *op. cit.*, p. 13.

59. E. Pumpian-Mendlin, M.D., "Omnipotentiality, Youth and Commitment," *Journal of the American Academy of Child Psychiatry*, Vol. IV, No. 1 (January, 1965), p. 2.

60. Hyman Weiland, "The Psychological Significance of Hot Rods and Automobiles to Adolescent Males," *Psychiatric Quarterly Supplement*, Vol. XXXI, No. 1 (1957), pp. 261–275.

61. Spafford Ackerly, "Late Adolescence: A Lying Fallow Period of Consolidation," *Conditio Humana*, ed. by Walter van Baeyer and Richard M. Griffith (Berlin: Springer-Verlag, 1966), p. 7. (One disclaimer needs to be entered here. Ackerly, Erikson, Allport, and others may be speaking out of a background of work with middle-class and upper-class young people. These youths tend to be deprived of the "wanderer's" rights which lower-class families may or may not take for granted as a part of the necessity of the young person to "get out of the nest" sooner. Poverty makes these finer subtleties a luxury in the face of survival necessities. Also, larger families among the poor tend to necessitate their shortening of the time of "adolescing."

Finally, the disadvantaged youth will often look upon "working his way through school" as an adventure in itself. The privileged youth may look on learning to "earn his own keep" as an adventure and look nonchalantly at a prepaid education beyond high school.)

62. *Ibid.*, p. 8.

63. *Ibid.*, p. 9.

64. *Letters of James Agee to Father Flye* (George Braziller, Inc., 1963; Bantam Book Edition), p. 50.

65. Witmer and Kotinsky (eds.), *op. cit.*, p. 5.

66. Alan Wheelis, *The Quest for Identity* (W. W. Norton & Company, Inc., 1958), p. 19.

67. Lewis Untermeyer (ed.), *Modern American and Modern British Poetry* (Harcourt, Brace & Co., Inc., 1955).

68. Gordon Allport, *Becoming: Basic Considerations for a Psychology of Personality* (Yale University Press, 1955), pp. 49–51.

69. *Ibid.*

70. Kenneth Harris, "Don't Stifle Your Students' Nonconformity," *National Education Association Journal,* October, 1966, p. 26.

71. Ackerly, *op. cit.,* pp. 12–13.

72. Antoine de Saint-Exupéry, *The Little Prince* (Reynal & Hitchcock, 1943), pp. 66–68.

73. Allport, *The Individual and His Religion,* p. 142.